D0954813

CULTURE SMART!
BRITAIN

Paul Norbury

Graphic Arts Center Publishing®

First published in Great Britain 2003
by Kuperard, an imprint of Bravo Ltd.

Copyright © 2003 Kuperard

All rights reserved. No part of this publication may be reprinted
or reproduced, stored in a retrieval system, or transmitted in any
form or by any means without prior permission in writing from
the Publishers.

Series Editor Geoffrey Chesler
Design DW Design

Simultaneously published in the U.S.A. and Canada
by Graphic Arts Center Publishing Company
P. O. Box 10306, Portland, OR 97296-0306

ISBN 1-55868-775-0
Library of Congress information available upon request.

Printed in Hong Kong

Cover image: Bakewell, Derbyshire.
Travel Ink/Andrew Milliken

CultureShock!Consulting and **Culture Smart!** guides both contribute
to and regularly feature in the weekly travel program "Fast Track" on
BBC World TV.

About the Author

PAUL NORBURY is a publisher, editor, and author who has written on international business practice and procedure, with particular reference to the Far East. He has specialized in publishing books on intercultural communication. Whereas in the past he has focused on explaining Asian culture to Westerners, in this book he uses his experience as mediator and interpreter to introduce his native Britain to visitors from abroad.

Other Books in the Series

- Culture Smart! Australia
- Culture Smart! China
- Culture Smart! France
- Culture Smart! Germany
- Culture Smart! India
- Culture Smart! Ireland
- Culture Smart! Italy (2004)
- Culture Smart! Japan
- Culture Smart! Netherlands
- Culture Smart! Philippines (2004)
- Culture Smart! Russia
- Culture Smart! Singapore (2004)
- Culture Smart! Spain
- Culture Smart! Sweden (2004)
- Culture Smart! Switzerland (2004)
- Culture Smart! Thailand
- Culture Smart! U.S.A. (2004)

Other titles are in preparation. For more information, contact: info@kuperard.co.uk

The publishers would like to thank **CultureShock!**Consulting for its help in researching and developing the concept for this series.

CultureShock!Consulting

We are all likely at some time to be dealing with other cultures—foreign visitors at home, e-mails from abroad, overseas sales agents, multicultural teams within our organization, or a new foreign management structure.

CultureShock!Consulting creates tailor-made seminars and consultancy programs to meet all types of corporate, public sector, and individual intercultural needs. It provides pre- and post-assignment programs, as well as ongoing "in-the-field" counseling worldwide.

For details, see www.cultureshockconsulting.com

contents

CONTENTS

contents

Map of Britain

introduction

Many visitors to Britain have preconceived notions of what they will encounter—and they are frequently surprised. Even those who speak English as their mother tongue can be nonplussed: Oscar Wilde described Britain and America as "two nations divided by the same language." The peoples of these islands are the product of a long and varied history. They can baffle, charm, and sometimes dismay those who have grown up elsewhere.

The Act of Union of 1707 that united the governments of England and Scotland, thereby creating Great Britain, was complex—nearly as confusing as the national game of cricket. For visitors, the character of the British themselves has always been a puzzle. Words like "complex," "enigmatic," and "idiosyncratic" come to mind, as do other epithets such as "reserved," "quaint," and "eccentric."

It is also true that for many British people there is still pride in the past and a kind of nostalgia for the "good old days"—a collective memory of the country as it was before World War II. Britain has a reputation abroad, not surprisingly, for being insular and "different." None of these stereotypes bother the British at all. As a people they are immensely inventive, reflective, focused, and tenacious—qualities that have generated some extraordinary outcomes, not least an empire that was the biggest the world has ever known, a monarchy that has endured for over a thousand years, and a parliamentary democracy that has been the template for the rest of the world.

Britain has produced some of the world's greatest literature, gave rise to the Industrial Revolution, was the source of most of the world's major sports, and has invented countless items of technology that have advanced the quality of modern life. It has won more Nobel Prizes than the countries of Europe combined, and has done more than any other nation to unite the world, first through its great trading empire, and then through the legacy of English as a global language. Frequently at the forefront of change, the British remain peculiarly attached to their past.

The following pages aim to help the visitor to understand something about the customs, values, and changing way of life of this remarkable island people who once ruled over a third of the world.

culture smart! **britain**

Key Facts

Official Name	The United Kingdom of Great Britain and Northern Ireland	Member of NATO, the EU, G7, G8, OECD, and the UN Security Council.
Capital Cities	London: the EU's largest city, with a pop. of 7 million.	Other capitals: Edinburgh, Cardiff, Belfast.
Other Main Cities	*England:* Birmingham, Manchester, Liverpool *Scotland:* Glasgow, Aberdeen *Wales:* Swansea, Wrexham, Newport *Northern Ireland:* Londonderry	
Area	Total area approx. 93,832 sq. miles (243,025 sq. km). *England:* 50,318 sq.miles (130,324 sq. km) *Scotland:* 30,297, sq. miles (78,469 sq. km) *Wales:* 8,021 sq. miles (20,774 sq. km) *N. Ireland:* 5,196 sq. miles (13,458 sq. km)	
Climate	Temperate	London temp. ranges from 36–43°F (2-6°C) in January to 55–90° F (13-32°C) in July.
Population	59,756,000, broken down as follows: *England* 49,997,000 *Scotland* 5,115,000 *Wales* 2,946,000 *Northern Ireland* 1,698,000	White: 92.1% Minority ethnic groups: 7.9% Princ. ethnic groups: Indian, Pakistani, Black Caribbean, Black African.
Family Makeup	Average members per household: 2.4	Pop. under 15: 19% Pop. over 65: 15.8%
Religion	Church of England, Churches of Wales and Scotland (Protestant traditions), Roman Catholic.	Principal minority religions: Judaism, Hinduism, Islam, Sikhism.
Language	English	English and Welsh in Wales.

Government	Constitutional Monarchy. No written constitution: the relationship between state and people is based on statute law, common law, and conventions. Parliament comprises two chambers, the House of Commons (elected) and House of Lords (unelected), and remains the supreme authority of government and law-making in the UK, despite devolved administrations in Scotland, Wales, and Northern Ireland.	
Currency	Pound Sterling	
Press	Broadsheets: *The Times, The Guardian, The Independent, The Daily Telegraph*, and *The Observer* (Sunday). There are five national "tabloid" newspapers.	Regional newspapers are published throughout the country, the biggest being *The Daily Record* (circulation 0.6 million) in Scotland.
Broadcasting	BBC-TV has two main channels, 1 and 2, plus six digital channels. Independent TV has various commercial plus digital channels. There are two principal cable companies.	Radio is still dominated by the BBC, but there are many independent broadcasters. Approx. 40% of households are connected to the Internet.
Electricity	240 volts throughout the country.	
Video/TV	PAL system	
Telephone	Britain's country code is 44.	Following deregulation, there are now around 50 service providers.

chapter one

LAND & PEOPLE

WHAT IS "BRITAIN"?

The visitor may wonder about the different names used to describe the country referred to as Britain, Great Britain, the United Kingdom, the U.K., and England (the latter still being used by much of the rest of the world, including the United States). Correctly speaking, Great Britain comprises England, Wales, and Scotland, together with all the offshore islands, including the Isle of Wight, the Isles of Scilly, the Hebrides, Orkney, and Shetlands.

The United Kingdom comprises Great Britain and Northern Ireland. The Isle of Man in the Irish Sea, and the Channel Islands, in the English Channel, between Great Britain and France, are largely self-governing, and are known as Crown Dependencies; but they are not part of the U.K.

The name "British Isles" is essentially a geographical term, and describes all of the above plus the whole of the island of Ireland, as well as the Isle of Man and the Channel Islands.

Britain is located on the westernmost edge of the continental shelf of Europe. It consists of two large and several hundred small islands that were separated from the European continent in about 6000 BCE. The mild maritime climate and gently undulating lowlands give the mainland an excellent agricultural base. The landscape becomes increasingly mountainous toward the north, rising to the Grampian Mountains in Scotland, the Pennines in northern England, and the Cambrian Mountains in Wales. The major rivers include the Thames in the south, the Severn in the west, and the Spey in Scotland.

CLIMATE

Britain's climate is often thought of as cool, wet, cloudy, and windswept. This generalization, however, fails to take account of the many regional variations in weather, or the microclimates that are found all over the country; it is also a fact that, increasingly, global warming appears to be blurring the distinctions of the seasons, especially the autumn (fall)—winter—spring period. The British weather overall is controlled mainly by a series of depressions from the Atlantic that move across or pass near the British Isles on account of the prevailing southwesterly wind.

Talking About the Weather

Given the considerable variations in Britain's weather both regionally and historically, it is no surprise that there is a great deal of "weather talk" among the population. Take the year 2000, for example, which began with the sunniest winter in England and Wales since 1909, followed by the wettest April since 1766, when records began. Parts of Scotland and Northern Ireland then had the driest July since 1929, before October saw rainfall records broken throughout the country. The fall turned out to be the wettest for England and Wales since records began, continuing into the spring of 2001.

Historically, there have been many recorded "freak" conditions. For example, on January 21, 1661, Samuel Pepys recorded in his diary: "It is strange what weather we have had all this winter; no cold at all, but the ways are dusty, and the flyes fly up and down, and rose bushes are full of leaves . . ." On the other hand, on a few occasions, such as in 1683 and 1771, the River Thames has frozen, providing an unexpected arena for skating and other amusements.

Britain tends to be cloudy and overcast. Despite its reputation for rain, the fact is that only about half the country has more than 30 inches (76 cm) of rain annually—except in recent years, when freak flooding has overturned the precipitation tables. The wettest areas are Snowdonia, with about 200 inches (508 cm) of rain, and the Lake District, much loved by tourists, with 132 inches (335 cm).

England itself generally enjoys the best weather overall, especially the southwestern part of the country, which benefits from its position in the path of the Gulf Stream (as do the Western Isles of Scotland). The coldest

parts of Britain are the highlands of Scotland. On top of Ben Nevis, the highest peak, the mean temperature for the year is around freezing point, while many north-facing gullies contain year-round snow. Air temperatures seldom rise above 90°F (32°C) or drop below 14°F (-10°C). As this book goes to press in the summer of 2003, however, a heat wave in Britain has sent the temperature soaring above 100°F (38°C) for the first time since records began.

WHO ARE THE BRITISH?

Politically speaking, all the peoples of the United Kingdom of Great Britain and Northern Ireland, including the indigenous English, Scots, Irish, and Welsh, those from former colonies, and the many others who have made Britain their adopted country, are called "British." On the other hand, it is essential to understand that the historic cultural traditions of the British, particularly the Celtic, Anglo-Saxon, Nordic, and Norman French cultures, remain at the center of the "British way of life."

The centuries of conflict that were finally resolved in the Act of Union uniting the governments of England and Scotland in 1707 (the monarchies having united in 1603) generated a profound and, at times, fiercely defended sense of separate identity. This is, perhaps, best demonstrated in the separate national football and rugby teams for England, Scotland, and Wales. The matches between England and Scotland are fought out with immense passion, above all because they are a matter of national pride. But overall, most people (opinion polls and ballots prove this) would agree that there is far more to be gained by remaining united.

Multicultural Britain
In addition to the indigenous cultures, Britain also has what could be called its "Empire"

cultures—principally from the Indian subcontinent (3.4 percent), together with Africa and the Caribbean (2.2 percent).

In all, there are in Britain today some 4 million people (7.1 percent of the population) from other ethnic backgrounds (or a total of 9 percent, according to the 2001 Census, which for the first time offered respondents a "mixed race" option). These new communities are not evenly spread across the country, creating a very mixed pattern of integration and cohesion.

For example, about two-thirds of all Black ethnic groups live in London. In Leicester, Wolverhampton, and Birmingham, there are large numbers of Indians, and many Pakistanis and Bangladeshis live in Birmingham, Greater Manchester, and West Yorkshire, especially in Leeds and Bradford.

More than four-fifths of the total population of the United Kingdom live in England. The greatest concentrations of population are in London and the Southeast, South and West Yorkshire, Greater Manchester and Merseyside, the West Midlands, and adjoining towns in the Northeast on the rivers Tyne (Newcastle), Wear (Durham and Sunderland), and Tees (Middlesbrough).

Following the passing of the Race Relations Act of 1976 (amended in 2000), which brought about the establishment of the Commission for Racial Equality, the government has actively promoted a policy affirming the multiracial nature of British society.

While such legislation is not universally welcome, it is generally accepted. The great cities are already largely multiracial in character, and life is all the more colorful and vibrant for it; but traditional town or village life in Britain is still very far from this.

Many regions and towns are associated with great English writers, artists, and musicians, such as Stratford-upon-Avon (William Shakespeare), the Lake District (William Wordsworth), Yorkshire (the Brontës), Stoke-on-Trent (Arnold Bennett), Dorset (Thomas Hardy), Worcestershire (Edward Elgar), and Liverpool (the Beatles).

THE SOUNDS OF BRITAIN

The history of Britain has left a rich archaeology; but it has also left a remarkable "voiceprint" across the different regions of the country, with a great variety of accents, dialects, and vocabulary that can differ, even within the same region, from village to village and town to town. With over 16,500 rural towns, villages, and hamlets in England, the majority having populations of fewer than 500, many language variables evolved.

If you link this to British history, and the story of how the Island "mongrel race" evolved, it is hardly surprising. Even when Chaucer was writing his *Canterbury Tales* at the end of the fifteenth century, he was drawing on a vocabulary containing Celtic, classical Latin, vulgar Latin, medieval Latin, Saxon, Jutish, Northumbrian, Norman French, Central French, Danish, and Norwegian! And since then, borrowed elements from the rest of the world have been added— from Hindi and Urdu to African-American rap.

Some visitors ask if there is a "correct" or "standard" way of speaking English. The answer is that for much of the twentieth century the BBC and other institutions tried to promote a "Standard English." Today, it is recognized that no such standard is necessary, and that regional accents all have their own innate value. Nowadays BBC listeners and viewers hear a variety of accents from all over the country.

Accents and Attitudes

In his play *Pygmalion*, on which the musical *My Fair Lady* was based, Bernard Shaw wrote that, "It is impossible for an Englishman to open his mouth without making some other Englishman despise him." This neatly sums up the old situation, but is hardly true today!

HISTORICAL LANDMARKS

The British character has been shaped by the accident of geography and two thousand years of history. Successive invasions left their mark, the native peoples jostled for power, and collectively the British burst beyond the confines of their borders on to the world scene. At the end of this section is a list of significant dates in British history, which provides a useful point of reference. First, however, we look at the early centuries in which the foundations for the culture and way of life of today's Britain were laid.

In 55 and 54 BCE Julius Caesar sent expeditions to reconnoiter Britain for potential resources and settlement. Nearly a hundred years later, in 43 CE, the Emperor Claudius duly set about the conquest

of Britain, which was followed by some 350 years of Roman rule over an evolving Romano-Celtic society. By the beginning of the fifth century, the Roman Empire was in serious decline, resulting in the virtual collapse of many of its outposts, including Britain. The remnants of the Roman army withdrew in c. 409 CE.

With *Pax Romana* no longer maintaining law

and order, Celtic Britain was soon at the mercy of marauding German tribes, the Jutes (Hengist and Horsa), the Saxons, and the Angles. The Roman-style civil governments, or *civitates*, that were left continued to beg Rome, in vain, for help against the invaders. Eventually, England was overrun and became a predominantly Anglo-Saxon society, with the indigenous Celtic peoples pushed to the extremities in Cornwall, Wales, and Scotland.

The eighth century, however, witnessed the start of a new wave of invasions. This time, it was the turn of the highly sophisticated Norsemen—Viking pirates from Scandinavia, especially Denmark—to wreak havoc and devastation, at least initially, on towns and villages along vast areas of the British coast. The greatest Viking invasion, involving hundreds of ships—the biggest fleet England had ever seen—culminated in the fall of York in 867. Over time, the Viking authority in many parts of England was firmly established. The administration of these areas became subject to what was known as the Danelaw. Place-names ending in –*by*, as in Whitby, and –*thorpe*, as in Scunthorpe, bear witness to their Viking past.

Today, the archaeological and cultural history of York is centered on an outstanding enterprise known as The Jorvik Experience, in the Jorvik

Viking Centre located beneath the old city, showing visitors the different archaeological time-zones, with moving models, sights, and smells.

The next major milestone was in 1066, when the last successful invasion of Britain took place. William, Duke of Normandy, defeated the English at the Battle of Hastings on the south coast of England and became King William I, known as "William the Conqueror." The story of the battle

is famously celebrated in the Bayeux tapestry, presumed to have been woven in Canterbury, and kept today in Bayeux, northern France.

Northern French became the language of the ruling classes for the next three centuries and French legal, social, and institutional practice greatly influenced the English way of life. When Henry II, originally from Anjou in France, was king (1154–89), his "Angevin empire" stretched from the river Tweed on the Scottish border, through much of France to the Pyrenees.

However, by the end of the Middle Ages, almost all the English Crown's possessions in France, after alternating periods of expansion and contraction, were finally lost.

England and Wales were brought together administratively and legally in 1536–42 during the reign of Henry VIII (his family, the Tudors, had Welsh roots). After the death of Elizabeth I in 1603, James VI of Scotland became James I of England, uniting the two monarchies. The political union of England and Scotland took place in 1707, under Queen Anne. "Great Britain" was now the entity we know today.

Britain's great overseas trading empire began during the reign of Elizabeth I in the sixteenth century with opportunistic acts of piracy against the enemy, Spain. It expanded at the expense of its European rivals during the eighteenth century, making Great Britain the world's unrivaled naval superpower in the nineteenth century. The parallel story of Britain's great social, technological, and cultural advances,

that have effectively created the modern world, has been the subject of many books. What follows are some of the milestones in the general sweep of British history.

Some Key Dates

55 and 54 BCE Julius Caesar sends expeditions to England (landing at Pevensey, East Sussex).

43 CE Roman Conquest begins under Claudius with 40,000 troops.

61 Rebellion by the Iceni people under Boudicca (Boadicea). Paulinus crushes the revolt after overrunning London and St. Albans. (Boudicca commits suicide the following year.)

122–38 Hadrian's Wall built to keep out marauding Scots, running from the Solway to the Tyne (partly rebuilt 205–208).

314 British bishops attend the Council of Arles, a fact that provides evidence of an organized Church in Britain.

406–10 Britain loses its Roman forces.

449 Landing of Hengist and Horsa. Jutes, Saxons, and Angles land in Britain and begin establishing the Anglo-Saxon kingdoms.

597 Roman prior St. Augustine is sent by the Pope to refound Christianity in Britain. He becomes first Archbishop of Canterbury.

664 Synod of Whitby chooses the Roman Catholic rather than the Celtic Church order.

789–95 First Viking raids (via Weymouth in southern England).

832–60 Scots and Picts merge under Kenneth Macalpin to form what is to become the Kingdom of Scotland.

835 Egbert of Wessex declared "King of the English."

851 Organized invasion attempt by 350 Danish ships. London and Canterbury sacked.

860s Danes also overrun East Anglia, Northumbria, and eastern Mercia.

899 Death of Alfred the Great, king of Wessex. William the Conqueror defeats Harold Godwinson at Hastings on October 14 and seizes the English throne.

1085–6 Compilation of Domesday Book, a survey of English landholdings ordered by William I.

1170 Thomas à Becket, Archbishop of Canterbury, is murdered by supporters of Henry II on 29 December.
Richard I, "The Lion-Heart" (Coeur de Lion), crowned, and sets out on the Third Crusade. King John is forced to sign Magna Carta at Runnymede, near Windsor. By protecting feudal rights against royal abuse, it placed limits on royal power.

13th century First Oxford and Cambridge Colleges founded.
Edward of Caernarvon (later Edward II) created Prince of Wales.

1314 Robert the Bruce defeats the English at the Battle of Bannockburn, ensuring the survival of a separate Scottish kingdom.

1337 Hundred Years War with France begins.

1348–9 Black Death (bubonic plague) wipes out a third of England's population.

1381 Peasants' Revolt in England.

1387(?)–94 Geoffrey Chaucer writes the *Canterbury Tales*.

1400–06 Owain Glyndwr (Owen Glendower) leads the last major Welsh revolt against English rule.

1411 St. Andrew's University founded (the first in Scotland).

1455–85 Wars of the Roses. Yorkists and Lancastrians fight for the English throne; the Lancastrians defeat Richard III at the Battle of Bosworth in 1485, and begin the Tudor dynasty with Henry VII.

1477 First book to be printed in England by William Caxton.

1534 Henry VIII formally breaks with Rome, founding the Church of England and setting in train the English Reformation.

1536–42 Acts of Union join England and Wales administratively and legally, and give the Welsh representation in Parliament.

1547–53 Protestantism becomes the official religion of England under Edward VI.

1553–58 Mary I ("Bloody Mary") supports the return of Catholicism and burns Protestant "heretics" at the stake.

1558 Loss of Calais, the last English possession in France.

1558–1603 Reign of the "Virgin Queen," Elizabeth I, and the Golden Age of the Tudors.

1588 Spurred on by Elizabeth I's famous rallying speech, "I know I have the body of a weak and feeble woman, but I have the heart and stomach of a king…," a smaller English fleet defeats the Spanish Armada.

1590(?)–1613 The plays of William Shakespeare are written.

1603 Union of the crowns of Scotland and England, when James VI of Scotland becomes James I of England.

1607 First successful English colony in Virginia starts three centuries of overseas expansion.

1610 Plantation of Ulster. James I settles Northern Ireland with English and Scottish Protestants.

1642–51 Civil War between King (Charles I) and Parliament.

1649 Execution of Charles I on January 30 at Whitehall.
The first and only regicide in British history approved by the people (Parliament).

1653–58 Britain becomes a republic, the "Commonwealth," ruled by the Puritan Oliver Cromwell as Lord Protector. He abolishes the Monarchy, the House of Lords, and the Anglican Church.

1660 The Monarchy is restored under Charles II (1660–85), hence the Restoration Period (the Anglican Church and the House of Lords also reinstated).

1662 Founding of the Royal Society (for the Promotion of Natural Knowledge).

1663 John Milton completes *Paradise Lost*.

1665 Great Plague—the last major epidemic of its kind in England.

1666 Great Fire of London begins in a baker's shop in Pudding Lane and burns for three days.

1686 Isaac Newton sets out his laws of motion and the idea of universal gravitation.

1689 The so-called "Glorious Revolution." A bloodless coup against the last Stuart monarch, James II, it results in his expulsion and the coronation of William and Mary. Resisted by Scottish Highlanders and Catholic Irish.

1707 Acts of Union unite the English and Scottish Parliaments.

1721–42 Robert Walpole is first British Prime Minister.

1745–46 "Bonnie Prince Charlie" fails in his attempt to retake the British throne for the Stuarts.

1760–1840 The Industrial Revolution transforms Britain.

1761 Opening of the Bridgewater Canal from Worsley to Manchester and the River Mersey (42 miles; 67 km); start of the Canal (transport) Age.

1775–83 Under the reign of George III (1760–1811) American War of Independence leads to the loss of the Thirteen Colonies. The Empire continues to expand in Canada, India, and Australia.

1801 Act of Union unites Great Britain and Ireland, governed by a single Parliament.

1805 Battle of Trafalgar. Nelson defeats the French navy. From his flagship *Victory* before the battle he sends the famous message, "England expects every man to do his duty."

1815 Battle of Waterloo and final defeat of Napoleon Bonaparte.

1815–1914 A century of expansion of the British Empire.

1825 Opening of the Stockton and Darlington Railway, the world's first passenger railway.

1829 Catholic emancipation allows Catholics to hold office legally and be elected to Parliament.

1832 First Reform Act eliminates a lot of "rotten boroughs" and increases number of those entitled to vote by about 50 percent.

1833 Abolition of slavery in the British Empire (the British slave trade as such having been abolished in 1807).

1836–70 Charles Dickens writes his novels, starting with *Pickwick Papers*; his last complete novel was *Our Mutual Friend* (1864); in the year of his death, 1870, he had begun *Edwin Drood*.

1837–1901 Reign of Queen Victoria.

1846 Repeal of the Corn Laws. Shift of power from landowners to industrialists.

1859 Charles Darwin published *On the Origin of Species by Means of Natural Selection.*

1868 Founding of the Trades Union Congress (TUC).

1907 Henry Royce and C. S. Rolls build and sell their first Rolls-Royce automobile (the "Silver Ghost").

1910–36 The British Empire reaches its territorial zenith.

1914–18 World War I.

1918 Women receive the vote.

1919–21 Anglo-Irish war. The Anglo-Irish Treaty establishes the Irish Free State; Northern Ireland (the Six Counties) remains part of the United Kingdom.

1924 First Labour Government led by Ramsay Macdonald.

1926 General Strike arising from Coal Dispute.

1926 John Logie Baird gives the first practical demonstration of television.

1928 Alexander Fleming discovers penicillin.

1931 National Government coalition formed to face economic crisis.

1936 The Jarrow Crusade—the most famous of the hunger marches in the 1930s.

1939–45 World War II.

1943 The world's first electronic computer, "Colossus I," built; used for breaking enemy codes in World War II.

1947 Independence given to India and Pakistan; Britain begins to dismantle the Empire.

1948 Britain's National Health Service (NHS) begins, offering free medical care to the entire population.

1952 The reign of Elizabeth II begins.

chapter two

SCOTLAND, WALES, & NORTHERN IRELAND

The visitor should be aware that in Scotland, Wales, and Northern Ireland, despite superficial similarities with their larger neighbor, England, there are fundamental differences in self-perception, sensibility, style, and culture. So when visiting these countries it makes sense to approach them with a degree of sensitivity combined with at least a nodding acquaintance of their history and distinguishing characteristics. We hope that this chapter will help you to do so.

INTRODUCING SCOTLAND

The Scottish Highlands and Islands contain some of the most spectacular scenery in the world. Britain's highest mountain, Ben Nevis (4,409 feet; 1,344 meters) is in the Grampians. Scotland accounts for approximately one-third of Britain's landmass, but contains only some 12 percent of the population (5.1 million)—a population that is gradually declining, which is a cause of some concern within Scotland. The chief cause is the demise of traditional industries, such as shipbuilding and fishing, and only limited investment in the new high-tech sector.

Scotland's two largest cities are Edinburgh (the capital, population 453,000) on the east coast, and Glasgow (609,000) on the west coast; the two other principal cities are Aberdeen and Dundee. The least densely populated areas of Scotland are the Orkney Islands (19,000) and the Shetland Islands (22,000).

One of the most famous places in Scotland is Loch Ness, said to be home to a "monster" ("Nessie"), which has captivated the imagination of the world for generations. Loch Ness is a major tourist attraction, and its secrets will no doubt continue to engage the world of science, literature, and Hollywood for years to come. At the time of writing, no monster has been found.

The next most famous place is probably the eight-hundred-year-old Edinburgh Castle. There have been strategic buildings and royal residences on top of the striking volcanic Castle Rock since the eleventh century, when it was home to Margaret, wife of King Malcolm III. It was later used as a military garrison and prison. The sheer rock-face and vast scale dominate the Edinburgh skyline and can be seen from every direction as you approach the city. The Edinburgh Tattoo, featuring massed pipe bands, is the principal annual event to be held at the castle, concluding with a spectacular fireworks display.

THE PEOPLE

Scottish culture remains vibrant, colorful, and homogeneous, with quite distinct traditions. The Scots have a strikingly clear self-perception and a strong commitment to their own way of life, despite (or perhaps because of) periods of mass exodus in the course of their history (see "The Clearances," below). For example, they were prominent in the colonization of the British Empire, providing manpower, skills, and expertise in the engineering and technology of the time that effectively built Britain and the Empire.

This was in no small measure due to a strong sense of survival, persistence, and resourcefulness, and a superior education system, particularly in engineering, the sciences, and law, which is maintained today. The "colonization" process is now essentially limited to Britain itself—witness the key offices of state in the Blair government, as well as the many leaders in British industry, the arts, education, the sciences, and the media who have Scottish roots.

Scottish Enterprise

The radical, nineteenth-century Liberal politician Sir Charles Dilke, who even went as far as advocating union with the United States (in *Greater Britain*, 1868), observed: "In British settlements from Dunedin to Bombay, for every Englishman who has worked himself up to wealth from small beginnings, you find ten Scotchmen."

Some of Scotland's Great Names

In letters, the writer and poet Sir Walter Scott (1771–1832) is probably Scotland's leading literary figure (see the Scott Memorial in Edinburgh), followed by the poet Robert Burns

(1756–96), who epitomized the national spirit and continues to do so. The annual Burns Night dinners and parties throughout Britain and the English-speaking world, which celebrate the poet's birthday on January 28, are testimony to the Burns "magic." Other great Scottish men of letters include Dr. Johnson's friend and biographer James Boswell, the novelist Tobias Smollett, the philosophers David Hume and Adam Smith, and the Labour leader Kier Hardie. The first edition of the *Encyclopaedia Britannica* was published in Edinburgh (1768–71).

Other great names include the essayist and historian Thomas Carlyle and the writers James Barrie (*Peter Pan* and *The Admirable Crichton*), Robert Louis Stevenson (*Treasure Island*), and John Buchan (*The Thirty-nine Steps*). The most recent addition to Scotland's list of writers is J. K. Rowling, author of the Harry Potter books.

Arts and literature continue to thrive today, and the Edinburgh Festival (in August) has become a world-renowned venue for all aspects of the performing arts; the Fringe, with over seven hundred productions, is like an entertainment kaleidoscope, covering the sublime to the ridiculous. Two other summer events, the Jazz and Folk festivals, are also highly regarded nationally and respected internationally.

HISTORICAL PERSPECTIVES

Scotland was never a country that lent itself to conquest, nor was it ever conquered in any permanent sense until "conquest" took place in a political sense as a result of the 1707 Act of Union. This merged the English and Scottish Parliaments into a single Parliament based at Westminster, thereby creating the new state of Great Britain, and with it the Union Flag, which was the result of combining the two national flags—the red cross of St. George and the blue diagonal cross of St. Andrew. (Interestingly, following the union of the Scottish and English monarchies a hundred years earlier in 1603, the first "union" king, James I, used the title "King of Great Britain" to signify the union of the kingdoms by one monarch.)

But, for some Scots, the historical relationship with England has been painful. The memory of some events have remained in the psyche. Most celebrated, perhaps, are the Battle at Stirling Bridge (1277), led by William Wallace (later executed in London), and the overwhelming defeat of the English by Robert the Bruce at the Battle of Bannockburn, near Stirling (1314), which effectively put an end to the attempts of the English King Edward I from 1296 onward to annex Scotland and impose English rule. This resulted in Edward III's formal recognition in 1328 of Robert the Bruce as Robert I of Scotland.

The Scots supported the Parliamentarians (also known as the Roundheads, because of the helmets they wore) during the English Civil War (1642-6), only later to suffer occupation, albeit briefly, under Cromwell's Commonwealth because of Presbyterian-Royalist uprisings in 1648.

There were many more uprisings, in fact, following the Act of Union in 1707. The most famous of these was led by Charles Edward Stuart, "Bonnie Prince Charlie," who after some success was finally defeated in 1746 at Culloden, near Inverness in the Scottish Highlands.

"The Clearances"
There is residual anger over the infamous "Clearances" of the Highlands following anti-Union rebellions in the early eighteenth century, when the Scottish clan system was destroyed by the victorious English. In the early nineteenth century a great many of the tenant farmers and their families were forcibly removed to make way for sheep farming on a major scale. Further clearances took place in the late nineteenth century, when sheep farming itself in many areas was superseded by deer forests. These clearances contributed greatly to the mass exodus of Scots to the New World, particularly to New England,

Canada (especially Nova Scotia), Australia, and New Zealand, and other corners of the Empire.

It is not surprising, therefore, that Scotland has sustained a strong commitment to the rights of the working man and therefore the trade union movement, especially in Glasgow and the Strathclyde region, and continues a vigorous campaign, principally through the Scottish Nationalist Party, for independence. But today there is little enthusiasm as far as most Scots are concerned for an independent Scotland (as the 2003 Scottish Assembly elections showed); instead, most Scots vote Labour, and Scottish MPs at Westminster contribute vital votes to maintain the Labour government in power.

The Church of Scotland

The Protestant reformer John Knox was largely responsible for the establishment of the Church of Scotland in 1560, which is Presbyterian in the way it is run—that is, by elders as opposed to bishops—and based on the teachings of John Calvin and a strict interpretation of the Bible. (Knox's *History of the Reformation in Scotland*, 1586, is considered one of the masterpieces of Scottish prose.) Like the Church of England, it is an established Church, and though completely separate also has the English monarch as its official head.

The Scottish Parliament and Executive

Elections for the first Scottish Parliament in almost three hundred years took place in 1999 and the new, highly controversial parliament building near the old royal palace of Holyrood is due to open in 2004. It currently meets in the General Assembly Hall of Edinburgh's Old Town. The Parliament has the Scottish Executive and the First Minister at its head, and 129 members (MSPs), of which the majority are Labour. It is responsible for the day-to-day running of Scottish domestic affairs. It does not have a second, revising Chamber, like the House of Lords at Westminster. In the 2003 Assembly elections, fewer than a third of the Scottish electorate bothered to vote.

The Scottish Parliament's responsibilities include health, education, local government, housing, economic development, civil and criminal law, transport, the environment, agriculture, fisheries and forestry, sport and the Arts. In these matters, it is able to amend or repeal existing Acts of the British Parliament and pass new legislation. It also has the power to adjust the basic rate of income tax by a maximum of three pence.

THE SCOTTISH ECONOMY

The principal elements of Scotland's economy today are the electronics industry, accounting for over 50 percent of Scotland's manufactured exports, offshore oil and gas, whiskey, tourism, forestry, fishing, and financial services. (The four Scottish-based clearing banks issue their own banknotes; these are legal tender throughout Britain, but are sometimes regarded with suspicion by traders in England.)

Whiskey

In Britain, the spelling is whisky. There are some ninety distilleries in Scotland, most of which are in the northeast, and in 2000 they produced exports to the value of £1.3 billion ($2.08 billion). Malt whisky, in particular, which is distilled according to age-old methods and some folklore, is relished and celebrated by connoisseurs around the world. Writers approach their task of providing critiques about malts almost as a sacred duty, and provide evocative descriptions and annotations in carefully researched reference books. Indeed, more than anything, whisky *is* Scotland.

The distilleries on Speyside are particularly well known and enjoy a very high reputation (some of the most famous being Macallan, Linkwood, Cardhu, Glenfarcias, Strathisia, Mortlach, Glen Grant, Glenfiddich,

Tamnavulin, The Glenlivet, Tamdhu, and Dallas Dhu). There are 116 classified single malts, divided into Highland, Lowland, or Islay. The blended whiskies are the most common worldwide, but malt whisky consumption is growing as drinkers discover the wide-ranging subtleties that exist. Has the water that goes into the making of the malt, for example, been filtered through peat or over granite? Is the shape of the still significant? Has the barley been home grown or imported? It's all in the "nose"!

Whisky wasn't always Scotland's top tipple. In the seventeenth and eighteenth centuries, for example, the favored drink was claret, shipped in from Bordeaux to Leith. Indeed, Robert Burns himself testified to the vast quantities that were consumed in his song, "Gae bring tae me a point o'wine." The tax on wine put an end to its popularity, and gave the cue for the old illegal stills to go public (and legal) and develop the high value-added whisky industry that exists today.

Of Dallas Dhu distillery, established in 1899, the distinguished connoisseur and writer Wallace Milroy offers the following information in his *Malt Whisky*: "Nose: Delicate touch of peat. Taste: Full-bodied, lingering flavor and smooth aftertaste . . . The entire distillery is now run by Historic Buildings and Monuments and is an excellent place to visit. An after-dinner dram available from the distillery and the independent bottlers. Also, the Scotch Whisky Heritage Centre in Edinburgh provides a comprehensive introduction to the whisky industry and its 'water of life.'"

THE BAGPIPES

Although known to the Egyptians and Romans millennia ago, there is no doubt that today the "sound" of Scotland is the bagpipes, and has been so for centuries. The earliest piping competitions took place at the annual Falkirk Tryst in 1781, when a Highlander could be penalized for wearing the kilt or playing the "warlike" instrument, as it was then considered.

There is no sound on earth so stirring and elemental as that of massed pipes. The band of the Queen's Own Cameron Highlanders and others can be heard daily at Edinburgh Castle during the Edinburgh Tattoo in August, and at other major public occasions such as Highland Gatherings and pipe concerts and competitions. In the old days, most clan chiefs boasted a personal piper—a tradition that gave rise to legendary piping families, such as the MacCrimmons, the MacLeods, and the MacArthurs. Towns, police departments, and Highland regiments have pipe bands—the best known being the Muirhead and Shotts, Dykehead, Glasgow, and Edinburgh City Police Bands.

Hogmanay

This is the Scottish name for the last day of the year, and also for the oatmeal cakes traditionally given to the children as they went from house to house singing carols. Now it is more a media event, and is all to do with partying and having a good time—televised live from Edinburgh by the BBC as one of the nation's annual festivities.

CLANS AND TARTANS

Scottish life and culture used to be split between the Lowlands or Borders cities, towns, and villages, where intellectual, scientific, and literary life was nurtured, and the Highlands, where social life revolved around the clan system, *clann* in Gaelic meaning children or family. Loyalty was paramount for survival since the clan chief was at once leader, protector, and dispenser of justice. (Still to be seen today are the gallow hills and beheading pits, which were common features of clan territories.) The ties of kinship created a strong and at times very powerful social unit. Clan feuds, popularized by Sir Walter Scott in his novel *Rob Roy*, were commonplace and frequently deadly. The Scottish monarchs tended to leave the Highlands well alone.

After the final crushing defeat of the Scots at the Battle of Culloden in 1746, sweeping changes to the Highland way of life were introduced with the Act of Proscription (1747), which outlawed the wearing of tartan in any form (including kilts) and the carrying of arms. In addition, heritable (clan) jurisdictions were abolished and even the bagpipes could not be played in public. In fact, anything to do with Highland life was deemed undesirable. The Clearances helped to sweep away the old Highland culture.

However, in 1782 the Act of Proscription was repealed, which led to the commercialization and standardization of tartans, with the first tartan pattern books becoming available shortly after. Historians note that George IV wore a tartan on his visit to Scotland in 1822, which gave rise to a nineteenth-century tartan boom, nurtured by Queen Victoria, who had a special fondness for the Highlands.

Today, a tartan exists for every occasion, whether it be for everyday wear, hunting, or "dress" wear. Given the advances in the weaving and dyeing industry, it is not surprising that tartan links to the historic clans have become increasingly stretched, giving rise to some 1,600 tartans and variations registered with the Scottish Tartan Society today!

GOLF

It is self-evident that golf—one of the world's oldest, most sophisticated, and most prestigious sports—has come a long way since the ancient game of *gowff*, which involved whacking a stone with a stick. The earliest mention of golf as a game that we would recognize goes back to 1457, when its popularity was so great that it (along with "futeball") had to be prohibited on Sundays because it interfered with archery practice. In 1754 a society of golfers was formed at the ancient university city of St. Andrews. In 1834, under the patronage of William IV, this became the Royal and Ancient Golf Club of St. Andrews, and the ruling body of the game in Britain.

FOOD AND HOME

The Scots are friendly people. They may be dour, cautious, and candid, and are certainly not given to as much laughter as the English, but they offer a warm and hospitable welcome to the visitor.

Traditionally, the Scottish diet was dominated by oats. A typical main meal would be "tatties and herring," which is potatoes with herring in oatmeal. The popularity of oats lives on today in porridge, oatcakes, flapjacks, and such delicious sweetened dishes as Atholl brose and cranachan, both of which contain oatmeal, with various additions such as honey, cream, raspberries, and whisky or Drambuie.

The national dish, haggis, is traditionally enjoyed on Burns Night, "piped in" by a lone piper. It consists of chopped offal mixed with suet, oatmeal, onions, and herbs, and boiled in the stomach of a sheep, which for years gave the EU some headaches, resulting in an "approved" synthetic lining now used instead. The haggis is traditionally eaten with mashed potatoes and turnips, or may be presented in a variety of imaginative and delicious ways; there is even a vegetarian version. Other favorites include the richly fruited Dundee cake, shortbread, beef, venison, and several varieties of smoked fish.

Choose Your Moment!
Scottish visitors would be aware of one old custom—if a bottle of whisky is opened for a guest it has to be entirely consumed before the household retires for the night—and would thus choose the time of their visit accordingly!

Home Life
The most distinguishing common features of Scotland's main cities are the late nineteenth-century tenement buildings, built by developers

and entrepreneurs. With eight or more homes (apartments) to a block, they housed the workers who labored in the mills and factories, shops and stores, docks and transport systems that produced the wealth of Victorian Britain.

The tenements were hardly commodious, but somehow the large families common at that time managed with one or two bedrooms (the second bedroom was usually more of a box-room), a front room (which doubled as another bedroom), a kitchen, and a bathroom. Heating, of course, was by open coal fires. A common garden area at the back was used for recreation and washing lines. One such home, at 145 Buccleuch Street, Glasgow, is open to the public. Housing one family continuously from 1911 to the 1960s, it is now a museum of tenement life. Once renovated and refurbished, tenements are now much sought after by the younger generation.

If you were in one of the leading professions— a doctor, a lawyer, or a consulting engineer—in Edinburgh, which is also considered the "snob" capital of Scotland—your home would be in one of the spacious and splendid Georgian terraces on the west side of the city.

The Edinburgh social scene is predictably very closely knit, and the lighter, more refined Edinburgh accent stands out in contrast to the richer brogues of Glasgow and elsewhere. People from Aberdeen, to the northeast, are sometimes said to speak the purest English in Britain, on account of their traditional "clean" and "clear" pronunciation of English, albeit with a very defined and rolled "r."

Edinburgh may see itself as Scotland's center of excellence, but Glasgow is the heart of the country. A vast, sprawling city, capital of the Strathclyde region, with enormous contrasts in wealth and poverty, it has great character and panache, and an amazing array of subcultures. Some of the downtown dialects are almost incomprehensible, even to other Scots. Glasgow boasts some of the finest specimens of Victorian and modern architecture, and has been recognized as the Garden City, the City of Culture, and the City of Architecture, which celebrated the enormous contributions its famous son, Charles Rennie Mackintosh (1868–1928) made to the place with his distinctive designs, especially his masterpiece, the Glasgow School of Art.

Also, Glasgow *is* football (soccer), epitomized in two teams, Celtic and Rangers, the former being the Protestant and the latter the Catholic football team (never confuse the two!). Both teams sit at the top of the Scottish Premier Football Division, and battle for first place on an annual basis.

EDUCATION

The Scottish education system has a number of distinctive features, including the structure and organization of schools, a separate system of examinations, and differences in the curriculum. Record numbers of students continue with vocational, further, or higher education; and, unlike England and Wales, Scotland offers a very supportive financial package to students going on to continue their studies, especially at university.

GAELIC

Scottish Gaelic is a Celtic language, akin to Irish. As a spoken language it is on the decline, with perhaps fewer than 60,000 speakers who are competent enough to use it as a first language. Most of these live in the Hebrides (where over 70 percent are Gaelic speakers) and Skye (about 60 percent), off Scotland's west coast. The main institution for Gaelic culture is the An Communn Gaidhealach, based in Inverness.

INTRODUCING WALES

In Welsh, it is known as *Cymru*, which roughly translates as "the country of friends." In English it is known simply as Wales—a land of chapels, valleys, and hill farming, and vast, empty, mountainous spaces. It is the land where there is a growing passion to speak the Welsh language and consequently where, uniquely in Britain, most official signs and notices are bilingual. Wales is also the land of the male voice choir—one of the signally beautiful things that emerged out of the dark and desperate era of coal mining and the iron foundries, which, mercifully, is long gone.

Not surprisingly, given the ethereal beauty of its geography and ever-changing climate, sitting as it does as Britain's front door to the prevailing weather systems of the Atlantic, Wales is also a place where the spirit can take time out to be creative. It acts as a magnet to writers, musicians, artists, and craftspeople from around the world. All this is encapsulated in the annual Welsh cultural festival, the *Eisteddfod*, where lyrical poetry is sung to a harp accompaniment and male voice choirs go for gold.

On Arrival

Visitors to Wales will quickly become aware that they are in a "foreign" country: the Welsh language is spoken widely—although is not so evident in metropolitan Cardiff—and appears on all road signs, public notices, and official buildings. Don't try to pronounce Welsh: it is full of consonants, and requires assiduous study.

Apart from some isolated areas where Welsh is the first language, everyone also speaks English and you will be warmly welcomed as a visitor. You may find aspects of local life, traditionally informed by a strict chapel Methodism, very parochial, and the people not especially enthusiastic about the English. But that shouldn't deter you from enjoying the rich Celtic culture and its traditions that are there to be discovered.

GEOGRAPHY

The most famous of the Welsh highland areas is Snowdonia National Park in the north of the country, which spreads across some 825 square miles (2,137 sq. km), with Snowdon (*Yr Wyddfa*), its highest peak, rising to 3,560 feet (1,085 m). But although the north is the most mountainous area, there are also delightful upland areas of central Wales. The River Severn, at 210 miles (338 km) is the longest river in Britain. The Brecon Beacons are the center of another National Park of about 500 square miles (l,300 sq. km). The Welsh mountains are important sources of water for Wales, and for major English cities such as Liverpool and Birmingham.

SOME HISTORY

Long before the Romans left Britain, Wales was an autonomous Celtic stronghold ruled by sovereign princes. But by the eleventh century, the emerging Anglo-Norman kingdom of England found it increasingly difficult to accept the breakdown of law and order along its borders resulting from the rivalry that was rife among the Welsh princes. William the Conqueror had himself addressed (without much success) what came to be known as the "Welsh problem," and in the second half of the twelfth century Henry II set up a system of "divide and rule" schemes involving small areas of jurisdiction whereby his famous, and often ruthless, Anglo-Norman Marcher barons held power in key places such as Chepstow, Brecon, and Monmouth. (The so-called Marcher barons were appointed to supervise the Marches, the boundary areas of England with Wales, and also with Scotland.)

Matters came to a head in 1282 when Edward I brought Wales under English rule by defeating the last Welsh prince, Llywelyn ap Gruffydd. This signaled the end of any hope of an independent country. Edward consolidated his position by building a series of magnificent and impregnable castles in strategic places across Wales. The sheer scale of the building project was breathtaking, greater than anything that had taken place in Europe before, or has taken place since. It was supervised by a master builder known as Master James of St.-George, and these castles, including Aberystwyth, Harlech, Caernarvon, Conway, and Flint, are some of the finest historic monuments in Britain

today. As one historian has since observed, nothing like this had happened in Britain since Hadrian's Wall. To further make his point about who was in charge, Edward I's son, later Edward II, was born in Caernarvon Castle in 1284 and declared the first English Prince of Wales. The eldest son of the reigning monarch still traditionally bears this title; Prince Charles was made Prince of Wales in 1969.

By the turn of the fifteenth century, Welsh resentment over English laws and administration, together with widespread poverty and economic hardship, brought the nationalist leader Owain Glyndwr (Owen Glendower) into open confrontation with King Henry lV. After some initial success against the English, Glyndwr was defeated by Henry and the Prince of Wales at the Battle of Shrewsbury in 1403. The Welsh may have been defeated, but before the century was out, blood ties linked them inextricably to the English monarchy.

With the accession of Henry VII in 1485, the Tudor dynasty came into being, bringing with it important Welsh ancestry. As a result, under Henry VIII, two key Acts of Union in 1536 and 1542 united England and Wales administratively, politically, and legally. This has remained the case until the present day; hence you will see references to the laws "governing England and Wales," while Scotland and Northern Ireland have their own legislatures and legal systems.

A referendum was held in Wales in 1997, as part of the Labour government's policy of devolution, to decide whether Wales should have a token independent Assembly with some control over Welsh affairs (the National Assembly for

Wales). The referendum attracted few voters (about a third of the electorate), with those in favor coming barely ahead of those who rejected the idea. Nevertheless, it may be seen in years to come as a turning point in Welsh history. Westminster continues to control foreign affairs, defense, taxation, overall economic policy, crime, justice, prisons, social security, and broadcasting.

COAL AND IRON

In the eighteenth and nineteenth centuries, the Industrial Revolution had a major impact in south Wales, where the iron and steel factories and the coal mines were concentrated. The capital, Cardiff, grew in the nineteenth century as a coal exporting port, and Swansea and Newport also depended for their prosperity on the surrounding industries as well as their position as ports in the Bristol Channel. Among the most famous steel towns were Merthyr Tydfil and Ebbw Vale. Over time, of course, all the valleys where coal was accessible attracted settlers. The coal was transported to the ports by railways and canals—most famously, the Monmouthshire canal to Newport, which opened in 1791.

THE WELSH ECONOMY

Over the last twenty years, the governmental Welsh Development Agency has been a model of its type and the envy of many, attracting over two thousand inward investment projects to Wales, worth some £14 billion (U.S. $22.4 billion), which in turn has secured over two hundred thousand jobs, of which some seventy thousand are in manufacturing plants owned by overseas investors.

Manufacturing accounts for about 25 percent of GDP in Wales, compared to around 18 percent in the U.K. as a whole. Wales is an important center for consumer and office electronics; optical and electrical equipment; automotive components and engines; chemicals, materials; aerospace; food; and drink. Not surprisingly, tourism and leisure services also make a significant contribution to the economy, together with (increasingly) call center enterprises—a far cry from the grinding and dangerous days of coal mining, iron, and steel.

THE PEOPLE AND THE LANGUAGE

The population of Wales is just under three million, with over half living in the industrialized south. Cardiff is the largest city (population 325,000), followed by Swansea (230,000).

In common with other Celtic cultures, such as that found in Ireland, the Welsh are very fond of theater, poetry, oratory, debate, and storytelling, and, as already noted, they love to sing—talents and preoccupations that are all represented among the great names of past and present.

Some 20 percent of the population are Welsh speakers, with Welsh being the first language spoken in the rural north and west of the country. Welsh is extensively used in broadcasting, most road signs are bilingual, and it is used equally with English in the Welsh Assembly. Since 2000 it has been taught as a first or second language to pupils throughout Wales; in addition, it is used as a first teaching language in some five hundred primary and secondary schools in Wales. The Welsh language has a unique, undulating rhythm, which has transferred to the accent of the Welsh when speaking English.

Some Famous Names
Twentieth-century politicians include David Lloyd George, the Liberal Prime Minister during World War I, Aneurin Bevan, who inaugurated the British National Health Service after World War II, and Neil Kinnock, who led the Labour Party in the 1980s. The names of the poet Dylan Thomas, the singers Tom Jones, Shirley Bassey, and Bryn Tyrfel, and the film stars Richard Burton, Anthony Hopkins, and Catherine Zeta Jones are world famous.

Welsh Crafts

Craftwork is a living tradition in Wales, and there are centers throughout the country where craftsmen and women demonstrate their skills and sell their products, from glassblowing to wood turning, from weaving to needlework, from pottery to pewter work. Wool from Welsh sheep supports a significant woolen goods industry; and Welsh slate, which is very plentiful and still widely used for roofs, has proved a resource for craftspeople in a variety of end products from nameplates to figurines.

INTRODUCING NORTHERN IRELAND

The rich Scots-Irish brogue of Northern Ireland is unmistakable. The planting of Scottish Protestant settlements and their Presbyterian culture among the indigenous Catholic population was always going to be problematic, as history has shown. The Troubles, as they are called, continue to be a burning political issue, and while security, as far as the visitor is concerned, is generally not a problem, there are flashpoints from time to time, and it is therefore wise to avoid obvious taboo issues, such as religion and politics, in conversation. But as elsewhere on the island of Ireland you will receive a welcome warmer than most.

The Province of Northern Ireland (often called Ulster, although it includes only six of the nine counties of the former kingdom of Ulster) is inextricably linked to the heartbeat of British history. Geographically, it is part of the island of Ireland, although at its closest point it is separated from Scotland by a mere 13 miles (21 km) of water, the North Channel.

After a bitter civil war, the famous national vote of 1921 offered the people of Ireland the choice between independence and self-rule, and remaining part of Britain. Twenty-six predominantly Catholic counties, including three from Ulster, chose independence, leaving only the six northern, and in those days largely Protestant, counties of Ulster to remain part of and loyal to Britain. For this reason they call themselves Loyalists (or Unionists).

Thus, there is a split culture in Northern Ireland, emanating from those associated with the Protestant tradition (principally Anglicans descended from the English settlers and Presbyterians from the Scottish settlers), who consider themselves British, and those associated with the Catholic tradition who consider themselves Irish. The two groups have a profoundly different mind-set. However, the current attempt at a peace process, begun in 1998 with over 70 percent of the people of Northern Ireland (and 94 percent in the Republic) backing what became known as the Good Friday Agreement, offers renewed hope. Efforts continue to be made to seek a compromise solution acceptable to both groups.

The Good Friday Agreement

This secured three objectives:

1. The establishment of an elected Assembly and Executive that is representative of both political traditions in Northern Ireland.
2. The establishment of cross-border bodies to foster and develop greater cooperation between Ulster and the Republic.
3. The commitment to expand and consolidate the relationship between the islands of Ireland and Britain.

GLIMPSES OF HISTORY

There is not enough space here to recount the long and complicated story of Ireland's history. Archaeological evidence suggests a brief period of Roman occupation two thousand years ago. English history in Ireland goes back to the time of Henry II (1154–89), who in 1171 landed at Waterford with four thousand men and the blessing of Pope Adrian IV. Within weeks he had ensured that all the Irish bishops acknowledged the authority of Rome, and most of the Gaelic kings paid him homage.

In the generations that followed, a new feudal Ireland emerged, based on the Norman English model, complete with castles, manors, walled towns, monasteries, and a French-speaking knightly caste, which, according to one historian, was " . . . utterly unlike the cattle-droving, kinship-based clans of the indigenous Gaels."

The Plantations

In the seventeenth century, Ulster became home to major "plantations" of Protestant settlers from England and Scotland, which, by definition, meant the confiscation of land. These were set up by James I from 1607 onward, following the failed Gunpowder Plot of 1605, which was blamed on the Catholics and which, in turn, gave rise to the hated anti-Catholic Penal Laws.

One of the most famous of these plantations was Derry, renamed Londonderry, because it was "adopted" by the City of London livery companies (these are charitable and professional associations that began as medieval craft and trade guilds, and accumulated great wealth and power). The livery companies took charge of building key areas of the city, from the town hall and the cathedral to top properties and stately streets, in order to attract a new Protestant upper class that would govern the indigenous Catholic population. Self-evidently, much of the tortuous and tortured modern history of Ireland has its roots in this so-called "Plantation" period.

In 1791, taking inspiration from the French Revolution and seeking to turn Ireland into an independent republic, a group of radical reformers came together, calling themselves the Society of United Irishmen. The French subsequently sent a fleet of thirty-five ships to Bantry Bay to help them win their freedom, but the plan failed owing to bad weather. The movement was suppressed after a failed rebellion in 1798, which led to Ireland being incorporated into the United Kingdom of Ireland and Great Britain in the Act of Union of 1801.

The pity of it was that William Pitt, the English Prime Minister, had promised various political concessions to the Catholics as part of the Union deal. But in the end, George III refused to sanction them, saying that it would cause him to be disloyal to his coronation oath to defend the Protestant religion if he did so. Pitt resigned in protest.

TODAY'S POLITICAL LANDSCAPE

Northern Ireland has a 224-mile (360-km) border with the Irish Republic, forming the U.K.'s only land boundary with another member state of the European Union. About half the population of 1.7 million live in the eastern coastal region, at the center of which is the capital, Belfast (population just under 300,000). Other major towns include Lisburn, Londonderry, Omagh, Antrim, and Bangor. There are twenty-six local government district councils, eighteen Members of Parliament elected to the House of Commons in Westminster, and, by proportional representation, three of the eighty-seven U.K. representatives elected to the European Parliament.

In the summer of 1998 the Northern Ireland Assembly was established in response to the Good Friday Agreement and as part of the British government's devolution program. It sits at Stormont, in Belfast, and its 108 members have full legislative and executive powers. In the fall of 2002, however (for the second time), following a failure to reach consensus on aspects of the peace process, including the contentious issue of arms decommissioning, the Assembly was suspended, and remains so at the time of writing.

Reunion with the Republic of Ireland continues to be an ideal for many Catholics in the north, and is the stated political objective of the radical Irish nationalist party, Sinn Fein, and the Irish Republican Army (IRA). Furthermore, the demographics favor the Catholic community, which is growing at a faster rate.

The Green and Orange Traditions

The most visibly challenging cultural aspect of the two traditions is dominated by the so-called marching season, which runs from Easter time to the end of September, and is essentially the preserve of the Protestant community. The biggest parades take place in July, marking the victory of William III, the Protestant King of England, over the Catholic forces under James II on July 11, 1690, at the Battle of the Boyne.

Such parades tend to be triumphalist in nature, featuring banners and bands, and are really a historical anomaly. They are mostly organized by Protestant/Unionist associations, including the "Orangemen" (who took their name from King William's family, the Dutch House of Orange) through their "Lodges."

The most visible manifestation of the "green" culture of the Catholic community is the wearing of the shamrock on St. Patrick's Day (March 17). Tradition holds that Ireland's patron saint used the three-petaled shamrock to illustrate the doctrine of the Holy Trinity. Shamrock is worn throughout Ireland on St. Patrick's Day, as it is in Irish communities all over the world.

THE NORTHERN IRISH ECONOMY

Although rural life is still a significant cultural factor in Northern Ireland, agriculture, forestry, and fishing account for only around 4 percent of GDP (compared to 1.3 percent for the U.K. as a whole). Manufacturing industry is around 20 percent (average for the U.K. as a whole), supported by new inward investment and growth industries such as computer software and telecommunications and network services. The new investment and businesses are valued as old industries, like shipbuilding in Belfast, appear to be in terminal decline.

Linen Emblem

Belfast was also famous as a center for high-quality linen, which was a significant part of the agricultural and manufacturing economies in the nineteenth century. Today this is remembered in the Northern Ireland Assembly, which features the linen or flax plant as its emblem—the six flowers signifying the six counties.

Some Famous Names
Irish culture, literature, and the performing arts in Ulster thrive as they do elsewhere. Well-known names in literature include Keith Baker, Colin Bateman, Jack Higgins, and C. S. Lewis; and the poets Ciaran Carson, John Hewitt, and Louis MacNeice; in the acting profession Colin Blakely, Kenneth Branagh, Amanda Burton, James Ellis, Liam Neeson, James Nesbitt, and Stephen Rea. In music, great names include the flautist James Galway, the singer/songwriter Van Morrison, the pianists Phil Coulter and Barry Douglas, and the blues guitarist Ronnie Greer.

chapter three

VALUES & ATTITUDES

Given the great diversity of the British people, it is fair to ask what their shared values are. The answer to this can be found by looking at different contexts—the historical ethnic mix of British society, traditional religious beliefs, the class structure, and the emergence of a new, multicultural Britain.

In reality, there is no such a thing as a uniform "British culture"—it could only ever be English, Scottish, Welsh, Irish, or, indeed, Asian British (and so on) culture. The English, however, are by far the largest of these islands' peoples, and are culturally dominant. The main part of this chapter, therefore, and much that follows describes largely English characteristics— although there will be many that apply to all.

Some "Virtues" and "Vices"

The English love nature and creativity, order and harmony, language and wit; and dislike pomposity. They are naturally curious, they are tolerant and fair, modest, practical, resilient, and self-sufficient.

But they can seem "superior," exclusive, and reserved. They can be too fond of alcohol and the "pub culture," and anti-intellectual. They can be stubborn ("bloody-minded"), and skeptical.

There have been a number of fundamental social changes in post-Thatcher Britain, the blurring of the old class barriers being one of them. The emphasis placed on individual fulfillment during the Thatcher years caused a huge expansion of entrepreneurial activity. This, combined with changing economic imperatives, resulted in a new culture of short-term employment contracts, which has led to very different notions, among working people, of loyalty, group responsibility, and perceptions of oneself in the community.

A SENSE OF IRONY

A British newspaper columnist once wrote that, after having been abroad for an extended period of time, it was an enormous relief to be back home in Britain and "on the same wavelength" as everyone else again. He put this down to reconnecting with the British sense of irony, one of the arteries of everyday communication.

It is true that much of what the British say is not quite what they mean. This is self-evident to the native listener, but with others it can cause misunderstandings. This particular aspect of the

British character does not seem to travel well.

Irony has to do with self-deprecation, with the "buzz" that comes from a tendency to laugh at oneself and one's situation, and an anticipation of constant, gentle amusement. Irony is a trigger for laughter, which, to paraphrase Billy Connolly, the British see as a form of free medication for body, mind, and spirit.

Not surprisingly, the British are not routinely polite to each other—a habit that can be oppressive in other cultures; and they don't suffer fools gladly. They are good "on parade," when they have to be, though they might grumble; but later they make merry, and usually make a good job of doing that too. Chaucer read the English character very well, and used irony, parody, and burlesque to great effect throughout the *Canterbury Tales.*

A SENSE OF TRUST

In his book *Trust*, Francis Fukuyama wrote of cultures that vary in fortune because of the levels of trust they enjoy and sustain; he cites Britain and Japan as High Trust cultures. It is certainly true that trust is implicit in the way the British manage their affairs, within local and central government, in their approach to law and order, including the principle that policing is done "with the consent of the people," in the way their judiciary system operates, and so on. Trust is taken for granted in Britain.

It is no surprise, therefore, that the degree of trust extended to each other in daily life is also remarkable, even though it is being seriously undermined by a rising tide of materialism and selfishness. The tradition of the "gentlemen's agreement" epitomized this philosophy of life and continues to be cherished, especially by the older generations committed to traditional values.

A SENSE OF FAIR PLAY

There is an old saying that "An Englishman's word is his bond." In other words, English society, which is not governed by a written constitution or a bill of rights, conducted itself on the basis of mutual trust and a sense of "fair play." For some, this is best expressed in the national game of cricket. Although incomprehensible to most of the rest of the world (except the few other countries that play it), cricket demands great skill and judgment, particularly on the part of the umpire, who must make key decisions on every ball bowled. It is all a matter of "fair play," and in fact the word "cricket," used in the sentence "it's not cricket," itself sums up the English idea of fairness.

In the late 1990s, the famous English cricket

umpire Dickie Bird, now retired, was asked "what is Englishness?" He replied with the following key words: "beer, honesty, bulldog-type virtues, royal family, cricket, the weather." He also used the phrase "not giving up when things get tough." Answering the same question, Jeffrey Richards, Professor of Culture at Lancaster University, observed, "a sense of humor" and "a sense of superiority towards foreigners—not concealed." Another commentator mentioned "a stiff upper lip"—a tendency to put up with a bad situation without complaining, summed up in the working-class phrase, "Mustn't grumble."

KEEPING ORDER

The English expression that "there is a time and a place for everything," suggests a need for order. This can be seen in the way people stand in line for public transport and other services; the order in the way the British conduct their civic and daily life; the requirement for "orderly conduct" at all times at public events—reinforced daily by the Speaker of the House of Commons, who calls (and sometimes shouts) "Order!" to silence over-excited Members of Parliament.

Not surprisingly, this desire for order is

reflected in the way the British have traditionally dressed. They still have a love of uniforms, especially those connected with the pomp and pageantry of a grand public occasion.

Even in everyday life there are many "uniform" traditions, in other words a need for uniformity in dress—often starting with school uniforms, obligatory at many schools, but particularly important at independent schools—hence the importance of wearing one's "old school tie" later in life at particular social functions in order to signal who you are and where you come from.

A SENSE OF IDENTITY

England, unlike Scotland and Wales, has no national costume. On the other hand, English customs and traditions involve a wide variety of costumes, from the pageantry associated with monarchy and great state occasions, through the distinctive red and black tunics worn by the Beefeaters who guard the Tower of London, to the traditional costumes worn by morris dancers and others at English country fairs.

So underplayed (or even undervalued) in England are the public displays of national identity—so highly prized elsewhere in the world—that England's national holidays do not include even the feast of St. George (the patron saint of England, famous for slaying a dragon) on April 23. In fact it generally passes unnoticed—whereas, as everybody knows, the celebrations by the Irish to mark the feast of St. Patrick on March 17 echo around the world. The English do not seem to feel the need for celebrations of this kind.

The Commonwealth Games of 2002, however, could have marked a turning point when, for the first time in living memory, the English crowds supporting the games at Manchester sang "Land of Hope and Glory" as the "national anthem" to hail the winning English athletes on the rostrum, instead of "God Save the Queen."

A Sense of Superiority

This has been expressed as, "The rest of the world have to keep telling us how wonderful they are—like the French, Italians, or Germans, who imagine that a perfect world consists only of French, Italians, or Germans. But the English, who will mix with anybody, don't need to broadcast how good they are. They just *know* they're the best."

A SENSE OF FAIRNESS AND COMPROMISE

Tolerance, fair play, and an instinct for compromise are fundamental qualities of the British character, along with a strong sense of justice, which draws on all of these and remains an abiding passion. Hence the existence of the enormous number of charities in the country, and the great amount of volunteer work done in the community.

In more recent times, however, the consensus has shifted from a sense of obligation to a new focus on individual rights and self-interest, and the concern for fairness that traditionally informed individual and group behavior is less apparent. In turn, this attitude has fed into "single issue" politics, which tend to engage in extremes, such as the Animal Rights movement or the ultra-right British National Party.

ROYALTY, CLASS, AND "HONOURS"

Despite all the changes to the social, economic, and legal landscape in the late twentieth and early twenty-first centuries, it remains true to say that to understand England and English ways (as opposed to Scottish, Welsh, or Northern Irish ways) you need to understand the class system. This continues to thrive. There are three main class divisions in England (which also apply in Scotland, but perhaps less so in Wales): upper class, middle class, and lower or working class. These are described in Chapter 7, Friendship, Family, and Social Life.

Until quite recently, everybody's perceived sense of "self" and their interpersonal relationships were informed by their view of their status within this class structure. The royal family is essential to the survival of the class system, because it defines one's position in society. Without royalty there can be no new titles, therefore no acquiring of status, and therefore no public confirmation of one's place in society (other than the hierarchy of wealth prevailing in the U.S.A.). Over the centuries republicanism has come and gone in waves, but it has remained a minority sport.

As far as social behavior is concerned, it is generally true to say that the further up the social scale one goes, the more one will find people observing the old-fashioned conventions and formalities reflected in the old saying, "Manners makyth man."

The "Honours" Lists

Britain has a public award system known as "honours," which confers recognition on worthy people for activities in all aspects of life, from serving the country as diplomat, politician, or civil servant, to making outstanding contributions to industry, sport, and the Arts. There are a great many different levels within the system, but it means that people from all walks of life can aspire to elevation. A highly successful and worthy Mr. Smith may even, one day, become Lord Smith. It is also a benign way of co-opting talented people into the Establishment!

Not surprisingly, the grading of honours is very finely tuned, from peerages down to minor awards. The Honours Lists, as they are called, are announced twice a year and are known as the New Year's Honours and the Queen's Birthday Honours. The New Year list is largely compiled by the Prime Minister of the day, advised by ministers and civil servants. The Queen's Birthday list, although also drawn up under advice from ministers and civil servants, has some direct input from the Queen herself together with her counsel. Titles are so broadly conferred today that some people feel their inherent value has become debased. There are also members of the Labour Party who would like to see the entire system abolished.

RELIGION

England in both tradition and practice continues to be a Christian country, but has significant representations of other faiths, especially Hindu, Sikh, Muslim, and Jewish. The Catholic Church continues to have the largest adult active membership of any Christian denomination, with over one million attending mass regularly.

The Church of England, however, is the only established Church in Britain. Its head, the Archbishop of Canterbury, is appointed by the monarch on the advice of the Prime Minister of the day. Its members are known as Anglicans, and the wider Anglican Communion is represented in a total of thirty-eight countries.

Under present laws, denominational schools such as Catholic and Church of England schools have the right to exist and be supported by the state in the same way as nondenominational schools. Easter and Christmas, the two most important events in the Christian calendar, are public holidays. At the same time, partly due to a more enlightened view of other faiths by schools and the media, festivals observed by other religions, such as Diwali (Hindu), Ramadan (Muslim), Vaisakhi (Sikh), and Passover (Jewish) are more widely understood and respected.

Churchgoing among Christians dropped dramatically in the last quarter of the twentieth century—to the extent that some observers at the beginning of the twenty-first century have questioned whether Britain as a whole has a majority of believers any more. However, religious organizations, including many multifaith groups, continue to be actively involved in volunteer work and the provision of social services.

In Britain as a whole, but in England in particular, the Protestant tradition has produced a wide-ranging architectural heritage. In a typical town, for example, you will see a variety of Protestant churches: Church of England, Methodist, Baptist, United Reformed, Plymouth Brethren, Salvation Army, Pentecostal, and Quaker (which are not so many compared to the three hundred or more different types of Protestantism to be found in the U.S.A.). As church attendance drops, or disappears altogether, many of these buildings become redundant and are converted into private dwellings or community centers.

More recent developments within the Christian tradition have included the rise of the charismatic movement represented principally by Assemblies of God and the Elim Pentecostal Church. Following significant immigration from the Caribbean from the 1950s, there is an increasing presence of Pentecostal churches.

A modest contribution to the spiritual dimension of life is provided by the BBC through its early morning "Thought for Today" broadcasts (in the Radio 4 *Today* program), to which spiritual leaders and others from different walks of life contribute by offering a short homily. There is also BBC TV's weekly *Songs of Praise* program, from different churches throughout the country and including hymns, reflective thought, and a celebration of the history of the place. A church continues to be the venue of first choice for weddings in Britain.

A SENSE OF DUTY

Although today one hears stories of individuals and groups demanding their "rights," the individual desire to take part in volunteer work for the benefit of others remains a particular and remarkable trait of the British character. There are over 185,000 charitable organizations registered with the Charity Commission for England and Wales. In addition, thousands of other groups get together in support of local community activities and local needs in social welfare, education, sport, heritage, the environment, and the Arts. Annual national events such as Red Nose Day (when thousands buy and wear a red plastic nose and do not mind looking ridiculous) in March, which is supported by the Independent Television (ITV), and Children in Need day in November, which is backed by a day-long program on the BBC, are the signals for millions of individuals, together with thousands of companies and community groups, to contribute money, time, and skill in entertainment or endurance projects to raise money for particular charities.

The "Sally Army"

Founded in London by William Booth in 1865, the greatly respected Salvation Army is one of the leading Christian organizations in Britain. It is the largest and most diverse provider of social services after the government. It also provides hostel accommodation, offering over three thousand beds every night for homeless people. Other services include work with alcoholics, and a family-tracing service.

The arrival of the National Lottery in 1994 has had a negative impact on the amount of money given to charities; on the other hand, a significant proportion of the Lottery receipts goes to "good causes." But there are worries that the decline in participation in the Lottery (under 50 percent of households) at the start of the new century is a long-term trend, to the detriment of the good causes.

In 1998 the British Social Attitudes Survey revealed that one in five people across the U.K. said that they had taken part in unpaid charitable work during the previous year.

HIGH CULTURE OR LOW CULTURE?

Britain's is not a structured "high culture" environment like France, Germany, or for that matter the Czech Republic, where the arts are the great benchmark of civilized life and behavior, against which all other levels of behavior are judged, and are all-consuming in terms of finance, media interest, and general protocol.

Remarkably, the arts in Britain flourish, despite insufficient support from the state, which, regardless of the political party in power, has invariably taken the somewhat philistine, anti-intellectual view that money will be found only if it is deemed to be in the national "cultural interest" at a particular point in time, rather than as a matter of course. The great British temples to the arts, such as the National Gallery and the Royal Opera House in London, are outstanding examples of their kind, but have always struggled to maintain their independence and obtain enough government funding to expand and experiment as they would wish.

The arts are often seen as divisive. Opera, for example, is widely perceived as being only for the rich, even though low-priced tickets are often available. The English love committees, so the government readily supports "quangos" ("quasi-autonomous nongovernmental organizations") such as the Arts Council, which is one of the conduits whereby the arts are managed and subsidized and appropriate compromises are reached.

DRINK AND THE WORK ETHIC

Traditionally, the British were not known for applying themselves overconscientiously in the workplace: most worked simply to earn the money to live. "Devotion to duty," and the very idea of "hard work" (with honorable exceptions, no doubt) are not phrases that readily come to mind. Not surprisingly, given the cruel exploitation of labor during the Industrial Revolution, it was the British who established the world's first trade union movement to protect the rights of organized labor. In today's climate of economic rationalization and "perceived value for money," this attitude has also spread to the Civil Service, once a model of efficiency, and the public sector as a whole.

It has to be said that part of the problem, even going back to Chaucer's time, has been the love of alcohol—mostly in the form of ale, or today's beer, with wine now making huge advances. In fact, up to the middle of the twentieth century, England had more bars (known as "public houses," or "pubs") than any other country in the world. It was said that there was one on every street corner in every town in the land.

The Industrial Revolution was "lubricated" with alcohol; the great national projects, like the building of the railways and the docks of London and Liverpool, could not have been completed without it. Today, drinking continues to be part of the English way of life. Some country pubs have suffered because of drinking and driving laws, but the pub continues to be at the heart of local communities.

As always, some excess is inevitable, with unfortunate outcomes such as vandalism and football hooliganism. In addition, surveys provide worrying signs that the drinking habit is now affecting more people at a younger age, especially teenage girls and young women.

HUMOR AS ENTERTAINMENT

Humor, as we have seen, punctuates daily life and covers many kinds of emotional responses. On stage, it is a popular form of entertainment, ranging from stand-up comedy to the "theater of the absurd"; from "other people's misfortunes" (slipping on a banana peel or walking into a lamppost), to "knock-about" or "slapstick" (with comics or clowns); from satire to parody; from self-mockery to the scatological; from farce to irony.

There is humor in cross-dressing—once a requirement for all drama in Shakespeare's time, but today found particularly in pantomime, where the classic children's shows, such as *Jack and the Beanstalk*, *Cinderella*, and *Puss in Boots*, require that the "leading boy" (the hero) is played by a pretty girl and the "wicked stepmother" (the comic character) is played by a bulky, middle-aged man—the "pantomime dame."

On television, comedy programs run across a similar range of humor, with the addition of sitcoms. Nowadays these include several highly popular American imports, including *Friends*, *Seinfeld*, and *Frasier*. Cartoons such as *The Simpsons* also appeal—and not only to children!

The World of Amateur Dramatics

The British are strongly self-sufficient. This fact, combined with an almost insatiable desire for taking part, has brought about a phenomenon known as "amateur dramatics." Up and down the country you will find local amateur dramatic societies putting on plays, musicals, and other entertainments. During World War II, British prisoners in German prisoner-of-war camps formed many such groups for the entertainment of themselves and others.

chapter four

THE MONARCHY, POLITICS, & GOVERNMENT

A BIRD'S-EYE VIEW

The visitor should know that Britain, which is regarded as the "Cradle of Democracy," is actually at odds with the rest of the developed world in that it does not have a written Constitution. Instead, laws and statutes are passed determining the nature of democracy and the freedoms enjoyed by the people as an ongoing process. Accordingly, legal justice is largely based on what is called the rule of precedent—in other words, what was determined in the past by way of legal ruling informs the present.

Also, the whole apparatus of the legal system is steeped in history, including dress and court conventions, which mostly date back to the eighteenth and nineteenth centuries; this is clearly something that pleases the English, and there is no sign of tradition being expelled. Except that in the summer of 2003 the government suddenly announced it was going to do away with the Lord Chancellor's office—the oldest and most distinguished Office of State in the land—and replace it with a Department of Constitutional Affairs. Other fundamental reforms of the legal system are also being considered, including the abolition of the House of Lords, the highest court in the land, to be replaced by an American-style Supreme Court. If you are in London, it is well worth visiting the Public Gallery when the House of Commons is sitting in order to experience the "Mother of all Parliaments" firsthand.

England and Wales on the one hand and Scotland on the other continue as they did before the Act of Union (1707) to have a different system of law (including the police), a different judiciary, different education systems, different systems of local government, different national churches, and different government departments. As we have seen, since 1999 Scotland has had its own Scottish Parliament, while Wales has had a Welsh Assembly, with considerably fewer powers. Northern Ireland has also had its own self-government, which was returned to it in 2000.

The World's Oldest Parliament

Interestingly, the world's oldest self-governing legislature is to be found in the Tynwald on the Isle of Man, which has been in continuous existence for over a thousand years. Originally under the nominal sovereignty of Norway until 1266, it came under the direct administration of the British Crown in 1765.

This recent process of "devolving power" also includes a change in London, where there has been an elected mayor and a separately elected twenty-five-member Assembly (known as the Greater London Authority) since 2000. Other metropolitan cities are looking to do the same thing, and, not surprisingly, some of the English regions, particularly in the north, and with strong encouragement from the government, have begun to consider the value and relevance of having their own assemblies.

THE QUEEN'S ROLE

The Monarchy is the oldest institution of government in Britain. It can be dated back to Egbert, King of Wessex, who united England under his rule in 829. The only interruption to it was the short-lived republic, or Commonwealth, established by Oliver Cromwell, which lasted eleven years (1649–60). This brief experiment with Republicanism was mourned by few.

The Queen's official title is "Elizabeth the Second, by the Grace of God, of the United Kingdom of Great Britain and Northern Ireland and of her other Realms and Territories Queen, Head of the Commonwealth, Defender of the Faith." The Queen is also Head of State of fifteen other realms, including Bermuda and the Falkland Islands, and fifteen Commonwealth countries (including Australia and New Zealand, the Bahamas, Barbados, Canada, and Jamaica), where she is represented by a Governor-General, appointed by her on advice from the ministers of the countries concerned and independent of the British government.

In legal terms, the Queen is head of the executive and therefore Head of State; she is an integral part of the government's legislature; she is head of the judiciary and commander-in-chief of all the armed forces of the Crown. She is also "supreme governor" of the established Church.

Royal Assent

When a Bill has passed through all its stages in Parliament, it is sent to the Queen for Royal Assent, after which it becomes an Act of Parliament and is part of the law of the land. Over the centuries, however, the monarch's absolute power has been almost eliminated, and the Queen acts on the advice of her government ministers. She gives audiences to her ministers (for example, she has a regular weekly meeting with the Prime Minister in which matters of state are discussed), she receives accounts of cabinet decisions, reads dispatches, and signs state papers. The U.K., therefore, is governed by Her Majesty's government in the name of the Queen.

POLITICAL PARTIES

Broadly speaking, the political system in Britain, as you might expect, is divided along class lines, although all parties would protest that they are founded on ideological principles. Thus, there is the Conservative and Unionist Party (Unionist is an inclusive word, but also refers to the Protestant Unionist parties of Northern Ireland that support continued union with Britain), which has a history going back over two hundred years. Historically, it saw itself as defending tradition, the landed gentry, and the middle classes; but in today's world of the politically uncommitted "floating voter," increased blurring of social distinctions, and head-on challenges from New Labour, which adopted many Conservative policies when it came to power in 1997, its appeal is across the cultural spectrum.

The Conservatives are also referred to as "Tories"—originally a term of abuse meaning bandits, which emerged in the period of Charles II. At the time, the other political faction was referred to as "Whigs" (today's Liberal-Democrats), meaning Scottish cattle thieves.

The Labour Party, founded at the end of the nineteenth century by the trade union movement, traditionally saw itself as the representative of the working classes. The new "Blairite" Labour Party sees itself as appealing, above all, to "Middle England"—the middle classes—which includes many "floating voters," but in so doing it has alienated increasing numbers of its traditional working-class supporters.

The third major party is the Liberal Democratic Party, formed in 1988 when the Liberal Party, which also has roots going back over two hundred years, merged with the Social Democratic Party, formed in 1981. The LDP occupies a position left of center, and appeals to the "high minded." It campaigns constantly for proportional representation in Parliament, and endeavors to make all decisions from the "moral high ground." However, the Liberal Party (or its successor, the LDP) has failed to gain office in over seventy years. Conservative and Labour have each held office eight times since World War II.

The Right of Self-Promotion

General elections to vote in a new government, which take place every four or five years, present an opportunity for the richly idiosyncratic nature of the English to display itself to the full, particularly in terms of the number of ridiculous and hopeless "minority" parties that spring up overnight. Most famous in recent years was the Monster Raving Loony Party, created by the self-styled "Lord Sutch," who offered an alternative to anyone disgusted enough with the political system to give him their vote. According to the rules, however, any party (or individual) that puts itself up for election must also put up a cash deposit, which is lost if it does not get a minimum of 5 percent of all votes cast.

ETIQUETTE OF THE "HOUSE"

It will come as no surprise to the reader to learn that Parliament, the seat of government in Britain, is sustained by a great many conventions that go back centuries. For example, during parliamentary debates in the House of Commons ("the House"), Members of Parliament (MPs) are not allowed to use each other's names; colleagues are called "My Honorable Friend" (or, if they are Privy Councillors, "My Right Honorable Friend"); whereas if they are opponents they are referred to as "the honorable gentleman (or lady)." There is no applause, and an MP can show only verbal agreement or dissent, hence shouts of "Here, here," which signify agreement.

Furthermore, there is a list of proscribed words in Parliament. Most importantly, you cannot call an honorable member a liar; but you could tell him you thought he was being "economical with the truth!"

The general manager of the House of Commons when it is "sitting," that is, in session, is called the Speaker. He or she determines who shall speak, and maintains control during debates by calling out "Order! Order!" when members become too noisy. Were the Speaker to stand up at any time because of serious disorder, then all members are obliged to sit down.

chapter five

FOOD & DRINK

British cooking has been much maligned. There are some ideas about it that may be partially true. For example, it has been said that the Puritans of the seventeenth century cast a shadow over just about every aspect of English life, leaving only a faint memory of the traditions of "Merrie England" that predated them. Food, or the love of it, may not have escaped this shadow.

Then, in the twentieth century, years of wartime austerity and rationing also had their effect, and people "made do"—in many cases ingeniously—with whatever they could get, or could grow for themselves. As a result, they became used to second-best for a while. The actor John Cleese, famous for his role in the sitcom *Fawlty Towers*, recalls how, for his parents, the only thing that mattered at the dinner table was that the plates were hot. The quality of the food was of secondary importance.

Despite the stories and the stereotypes, British food, at its best, has always been wonderful. The fertile land and temperate climate, suitable for both agriculture and livestock, yielded fine quality meats, game, crops of cereals and vegetables, and an abundance of delicious fruits. Surrounded by water, Britain had plentiful stocks of a great variety of fish and seafood. Trade with countries all over the world brought hot, mild, and aromatic spices, and welcome "new" foods such as potatoes, oranges, and pineapples. Britain had all the ingredients, and became skilled at preparation, producing a great variety of cheeses, smoked and cured meats and fish, along with its own favorite dishes such as roast meats, poultry, and game, nourishing soups and gently simmered stews, Yorkshire pudding, steak and kidney pie, Lancashire hotpot, fruit pies and steamed puddings. British beer, cider, and "Scotch" are well known for their quality. Sometimes British food has been described as "bland," but this was, and still is, alleviated by the use of hot, sharp, or spicy additions—mustard, vinegar, horseradish, pepper, pickles, and chutneys.

What lost Britain its reputation as a food-loving nation was, primarily, the food that was available in institutions and restaurants, which for many years, until the 1960s, generally lacked the imagination and drive to produce the kinds of meals to tempt people to eat out more than they had to. The British did not have a strong tradition of dining out for pleasure. Then things started happening: people wanted to eat out more, and demanded something better. Gradually, more restaurants opened up in the cities, and with this added competition and impetus the whole restaurant culture started to improve.

Then food programs began to appear on television, and now Britain enjoys several TV and radio programs each week devoted to the theme of food—growing it, preparing it, cooking it, and eating it. The world media explosion in this area is a phenomenon. Indeed, cookbooks have for some time outsold the Bible.

Today, restaurants in London and the major cities serve English and international cuisine to the highest standards. Eating out is now much more common, driven in part by increased personal wealth and the fast-food culture of youth, but also by the tendency among busy professional people not to cook very much at home, preferring after a long day's work to relax over a meal cooked by someone else.

This "discovery" of the taste and variety of food has also seen a huge growth in Britain's Indian and Chinese restaurants—Indian being the biggest "foreign" food of choice—so much so, that an annual competition for the finest Indian cook in the land has been celebrated on television for a number of years, and it has been said that Britain's favorite food is chicken *tikka masala*!

The "Fish and Chips" Story

The British love freshly made chips from real potatoes, which for the *aficionados* are very superior to the processed "French fries" served by the fast-food chains. Fish-and-chip shops as we know them today first appeared in the 1860s, and expanded rapidly, thanks to the first steam trawlers that quickly brought in quantities of fish from the North Atlantic and the waters around Norway and Iceland. Their clientele was the massive workforce employed by Britain's ever-expanding industries.

The National Federation of Fish Friers (established in 1913) represents the largest take-out food trade in Britain, involving over eight thousand fish-and-chip shops around the country. These continue to thrive in cities, towns, and villages, wherever there is a demand.

The traditional favorite fish is cod, although it is now the most expensive because of diminishing fish stocks, and haddock and plaice follow in popularity, along with local fish. The "chippy" will also sell you such alternatives as chicken, steak or chicken pies, or sausages, all with chips—or, indeed, just chips on their own. Always on hand, for any or all of these, are salt and vinegar—essential flavorings for a true fish-and-chip meal—or tomato ketchup or brown sauce. Fish and chips were traditionally wrapped in newspaper; today's hygiene laws insist on approved paper and/or paper boxes.

MEALS OF THE DAY

The Great British Breakfast

Hotels, guesthouses, and cafés throughout the country continue to serve a "full English breakfast" to those who want it. You will be offered fruit juice or cereals, and then some or all of the following, most of which are fried or grilled (broiled): bacon, eggs, sausages, tomatoes, mushrooms, kidneys, black pudding, and baked beans, eaten with toast and butter. To this challenging plateful, those who are sauce-dependent may also add tomato ketchup or "brown sauce." The meal is completed with more toast, butter, and marmalade, and tea or coffee.

Home Comfort

The famous brown sauce is HP Sauce, which has a ketchup-type consistency; those who use it like its "bite"—the ingredients include malt, tomatoes, molasses, and vinegar. It is apparently consumed in the highest circles: HP Sauce is honored by a Royal Warrant!

Porridge or cold cereals, eggs cooked in any way, ham, smoked fish, such as kippers (actually smoked herrings), or kedgeree—a rice and smoked haddock dish, a tradition left from the days of the British in India—are all good British breakfast fare. There is always the "Continental" breakfast, consisting of orange juice, bread rolls, toast, or croissants, with jam, and tea or coffee.

These days, most people do not eat the full English breakfast, preferring a quicker and lighter meal of cereals and toast, at any rate during the week. What continues to survive, however, is traditional English marmalade. Made from oranges (sometimes other citrus fruits) and sugar, this is available in different versions, from a sweet, jelly-type preserve to a thick, dark variety incorporating chunks of cooked orange peel. Many people make their own marmalade once a year, usually in January, when the bitter Seville oranges from Spain are available.

Lunch—and Brunch

Some families (mostly northern or working class) refer to the midday meal as "dinner," as do schools throughout the land. For the middle and upper classes, however, the midday meal is "lunch."

Then there is "brunch," which replaces breakfast and lunch, typically on weekends when you have not had to get up early, or have already been out for a swim or a jog. It is a relaxed, informal meal of whatever you fancy.

Lunch for working people during the week tends to be of the "soup, sandwich, or salad" variety. It is usually a light meal, though restaurants serve three courses for those who want them. Children would usually have their main meal of the day at this time.

A traditional English Sunday lunch typically has just two courses: the "main" course—usually meat or poultry (lamb, beef, pork, or chicken), normally roast, or perhaps slowly cooked in a casserole, accompanied by potatoes and probably two other vegetables. Over the roast meat is poured gravy, made from the meat juices, or today often from an instant mix. The second course may be called "pudding," "sweet," or "dessert," and is often some kind of pastry in the form of a tart or pie, filled with fruit; or even an old-style English dish such as sponge or bread-and-butter pudding. Over this may be poured cream or custard, a sweet sauce, traditionally made from eggs, sugar, and milk, flavored with vanilla, but nowadays often made from a powder or ready-made from a tin. In the health-conscious modern world, cheese and fruit are often eaten as an alternative to "pudding."

Tea

The Victorians instituted the custom of "tea," taken in the mid-to-late afternoon, which was tea to drink, plus a generous array of bread and butter, sandwiches, cakes, and tarts. "High tea" was a simple cooked meal for children at about 5:00 p.m., their last meal of the day. Some families continue the tradition of a substantial tea occasionally; many people sit down to tea and cake on weekend afternoons, and at its most basic level "tea" consists of just a cup of tea at 4:00 p.m. A typical West Country tea includes scones with jam and the specialty of the area, clotted cream. With homemade ingredients, this is a great treat, and is available all over Devon and Cornwall, and often, now, elsewhere.

"Tea" can also mean an early evening meal for working-class families, which, in fact, is supper—the basic evening meal—for everyone else. If you are invited to tea, the clue is usually in the time of the appointment. If in doubt, ask.

Supper or Dinner?

Supper is a simple family meal eaten at any time in the evening that is convenient. During the week it may consist of a cooked dish, such as lamb chops, cottage pie (minced lamb is the main ingredient, topped with mashed potatoes and cooked in the oven), or, these days, pasta, followed by cheese and fruit. If there is more time to spend on preparation, supper may be a more elaborate meal, but the name implies informality.

The word "dinner" usually describes a more formal evening meal, typically at 8:00 or 8:30 p.m, and involving guests or dining out in a restaurant. It consists of three or more courses, and a special effort would be made both in the preparation of the food and in the table setting. It will usually be preceded by an alcoholic drink—spirits or wines—and there will be wine with the meal, perhaps a different one with each course.

INVITATIONS

Invitations to a meal in someone's house, even "dinner," will usually mean a relaxed, lighthearted occasion. More often than not these days, men (particularly younger men) do not wear business suits or ties on these occasions, but they would probably have changed into something smart but casual. Women probably wear elegant but comfortable rather than very glamorous evening clothes (which they might wear for a "black tie" event).

It is usual to take a gift, such as flowers, a box of chocolates, or wine. These do not have to be very expensive, but they should be attractive and of good quality. Do not buy flowers from a gas station! The wine may not be opened, if particular wines have been chosen to go with the meal, but it will be appreciated.

It is polite to send a short note of thanks after such an occasion. Some people prefer to telephone the following day. Do one or the other.

TABLE MANNERS

A French saying suggests that, "While the English have good table manners, the French know how to eat." It is indeed a fact that while the Englishman attempts to push peas on to his fork, the Frenchman turns the fork upside down and uses it more as a spoon, thus accelerating the process of eating and enjoying—albeit without scoring highly on etiquette.

The British continue to use a knife and fork in the traditional way. Both are held while eating, the fork, with the prongs facing down, in the left hand, and the knife in the right, and in polite circles they are rested on the plate between mouthfuls, or for a break for conversation. Some young people are adopting the American habit of cutting up all their food first and then eating it with just the fork; though traditionalists view this as "not correct." If nothing on the plate requires cutting, then it is acceptable to use only a fork, held in the right hand.

Unlike the French custom, English children were traditionally brought up to rest their hands in their lap; later you were allowed to put your wrists on the table; but putting your elbows on the table, and, worst of all, resting your chin on your hands, were definitely not allowed. The idea was that you should not flop about lazily over the table, and this sort of behavior would elicit the remark, "Do you feel ill? Would you like to lie down?" Nowadays these manners are less strictly adhered to, except on formal occasions.

EATING OUT
Given the much more liberal attitude to dress when eating out, it is important to be sure whether or not the establishment you are going to insists that men wear a tie. A tie continues to be demanded by traditional London clubs, such as the Garrick, the Reform, and the Athenaeum.

Usually, when you are sent an invitation to a formal lunch or dinner, the dress code will be noted on the card, for example, "lounge suit," or "black tie," which means "dinner jacket" (tuxedo).

This code will automatically determine the dress code for the women.

Food on Your Plate—The Unwritten Rule

The British never cease to be amazed at the quantities of food served in America; equally, American visitors to Britain are often astonished at the small amounts of food that are put on their plates. In Britain, the rule used to be to eat everything on the plate, whether you or somebody else had put it there, as it was thought to be wasteful to leave anything uneaten. Now this has relaxed somewhat—if it's too much, leave it— but only in a restaurant, not in someone's house. If you are not very hungry, ask for a small helping.

The English and Service

Visitors should understand that basically the English today do not like serving others: it is seen as faintly demeaning, which perhaps is a legacy from the rigid class structure of the old days. The situation is not helped by the fact that the service industry as a whole is also the lowest-paid sector in Britain.

In other societies there is no such baggage from the past, and service is seen as something positive. Thus, it is often foreign workers who serve in the hotels, restaurants, and pubs in the major city centers. Young Australians and others using the opportunity of "work experience" visas in Britain are everywhere, usually offering service with a smile. There are also increasing numbers of visitors and immigrants from the former Eastern Bloc countries, anxious to practice their English and earn some money.

Paradoxically, there has also been a degree of rehabilitation of the service industry through a resurgence of interest in becoming a housekeeper, nanny, or butler, as more and more couples, with both partners pursuing professional careers, find they cannot cope without such help.

TIPPING

Traditionally, a tip of 10 percent, or slightly more, has been left for the waiter or waitress, regardless of the quality of food or service. It is an easy policy just to stick to this, particularly in a formal situation. But, increasingly, there has been a move against such automatic generosity, particularly among younger people. In the final analysis, you make your own decision, although good manners dictate that whatever you do, particularly if you are entertaining guests, you should not embarrass anybody. Sometimes a "service" charge is added to the bill, which solves the problem if you are prepared to pay it, as most people do.

THE PUB

Despite the rigorous drunk-driving laws, for many British people the pub continues to be the center of their social lives—amply demonstrated in the ongoing soaps of *Coronation Street* and *Eastenders.* Typically, people will pop in for "a quick one," which means a pint of beer; or "a swift half," which also means a pint of beer! Some serious drinking men spend the evening there, propping up the bar.

Pubs often have interesting old names that in some way reflect their history, like the Queen's Arms, the Woolpack, the Red Lion, the White Horse, the Eight Bells, the Victoria, the Green Man, the Ship Inn, the Boot and Flogger, the Bunch of Grapes. The variations are endless, and typically you will find the pub's name painted on a sign swinging near the front door on a post nearby. The Tabard in Southwark, London, for example, was mentioned by Chaucer in the *Canterbury Tales* six hundred years ago, and Ye Olde Cheshire Cheese, in Fleet Street, London, was frequented by some of England's literary giants, including Samuel Johnson, Oliver Goldsmith, and Charles Dickens.

As part of the rise of youth culture in Britain in the 1990s, some pubs were rebranded to appeal to smart and well-off young singles. Some of the old-fashioned names, such as Pig and Whistle or Royal Oak, went, and the pubs were refurbished with a "cool" new look; one of these new chains is called the Slug and Lettuce, in a tongue-in-cheek echo of the old names.

The most enduring image of the pub, however, is that of the country pub, which continues to be the heart of village life. Some have been there for hundreds of years; some have thatched roofs with wisteria or roses growing around the doorway. There are blazing log fires in winter, and an attractive garden to sit in for the summer months. These can be delightful, welcoming places, with "regulars" at the bar who are often only too happy to chat with visitors.

Traditional English beer has made a big comeback in recent years, sufficient to encourage the establishment of many new small breweries to be set up to serve their local area. Brewed from malt and hops, it is not refrigerated like other beers, which is why those who do not know when it is at its best (cooled but not chilled) criticize it for being "warm" beer, in contrast to the sometimes teeth-chilling temperature of pressurized or cask beer—principally lager, the lighter Continental beer, favored by football supporters, hence the name "lager louts" given to those who overindulge and then go on the rampage. One of the most famous darker bitter beers is Newcastle Brown, drunk mostly in the northeast of England where it is made, and favored by football supporters and many others.

If you go into a pub and ask for "a pint of best" you will be served with what the publican rates as "best bitter"; these days, though, there is usually a choice of several English beers, possibly including a local brew, plus Continental-style lagers. There is also "mild" beer, drunk mostly in the Midlands, which is what its name suggests—a beer brewed from hops but not as sharp as bitter, and softer on the palate.

Public and Saloon Bars

Many pubs continue to be divided into sections, such as the public bar, which is thought to be noisier, more "working class," and where the beer used to be perhaps a penny a pint cheaper than in the neighboring saloon bar, which is meant to be quieter and more salubrious. There is sometimes a smaller room called a "snug," where there may be an open fire. On the other hand, many pubs have now lost all the dividing walls in favor of one large drinking area for everyone.

Country pubs in some places have preserved some of the traditional "Olde England" games, such as "bat-and-trap" (found in Kent), which have been played for hundreds of years, or "shove ha'penny." Pub games continue to be very popular, especially darts, and quizzes, both of which are frequently organized on a competitive basis.

Food is another essential component of the pub scene; once pub food was limited to very basic and cheap fare like pie or sausage and chips, or cheese and pickle ("Ploughman's Lunch" is now a much more elaborate version of this, with fresh bread and salad). Today is it recognized that people want good quality food, and in most pubs there is now a much greater choice at reasonable prices. Some establishments have set out to offer restaurant-quality cuisine, and from this have created a new style of "pub culture."

Licensing Laws

The minimum age for drinking alcohol in Britain is eighteen, and the minimum age for entering a public bar (for consuming nonalcoholic drinks) is fourteen, but only if accompanied by an adult. Pubs that serve lunches may show families with children into a special dining room.

The government, however, continues to review licensing laws. "Opening hours," as they are called, used to be strictly observed: from 11:00 a.m. until 2:30 p.m., and from 5:30 p.m. until 11:00 p.m.

(and a shorter time on Sundays). Now, publicans are free to stay open all day and all night if they wish; but outside city centers the old closing hours tend to prevail.

Typically, those serving in a pub will sound a bell at least ten minutes before closing so that last orders can be taken. Extension to the licensing laws can be granted by the local magistrate if a publican can demonstrate there is a justifiable special occasion, such as a World Cup match, or a spectacular royal wedding, which can be viewed on the pub's television.

WINE BARS

A more recent addition to the drinking scene is the wine bar. These are generally found in the city centers. Many of them are very attractive places, some being refurbishments of old pubs, some ultramodern. Most of their clients are professional people having a quick lunch, or a more leisurely supper, and these places provide a good environment to meet a friend for a casual meal. They offer a variety of interesting wines, and usually very good food. Wine is not compulsory! Soft drinks and coffee are also available.

TIME OUT

For the British today, the focus on leisure and pleasure is a major preoccupation wonderfully summed up in the saying "TGIF"—"Thank God It's Friday!" Indeed, even on a Monday, with the previous weekend just past, broadcasters and the printed media are already heralding the joys to come for the following weekend, creating a seamless year-round perception that life is all to do with having a ball—just a pity there is the work thing getting in the way!

The cultural scene is certainly vibrant, and there has been a renaissance in the public interest in art galleries and museums of all kinds, with new institutions, such as the Tate Modern in London, springing up in metropolitan centers across the country—in part thanks to proceeds from the National Lottery.

The British love of language continues to find expression in theaters large and small (although London's West End has suffered since the terrorist attacks on New York on September 11, 2001), including local amateur dramatic societies, as well as in summer-season variety shows (including comedians, singers, and magicians) in the country's leading coastal resorts. The pantomime (see page 81), a unique children's entertainment in the Christmas vacation period, also flourishes.

POMP AND PAGEANTRY

The ceremonials of great public occasions continue to exert a hold on the imagination of the British, and are as much an attraction for them as for visitors from abroad. The State Opening of Parliament, for example, is a grand form of public theater. The Queen travels in a magnificent, horse-drawn state coach, dressed in her royal robes, and delivers a speech from the throne of the House of Lords. Around her the assembled ranks of lords, ladies, judges, and officers of the House are arrayed in splendid ermine-lined red robes, gowns, or uniforms, the military in the dress uniforms of their regiments with all medals on display, and the members of "the other place" (the House of Commons) in formal "morning suits."

Especially impressive is the spectacular Trooping the Colour, when the Queen, as Commander-in-Chief of the Armed Forces, accepts her new regiment of guards, in full dress uniform, to mark her "official birthday" on the second Saturday in June. Other fine sights include the procession of the Judiciary to the Law Courts of the Old Bailey in London, at the start of a new law term; and other state occasions when the Queen rides in one of the luxurious, horse-drawn carriages along the Mall, with guards on horseback in attendance.

WHERE TO GO AND WHAT TO DO

London is a world center for the arts. Its world-class museums and art galleries include the National Gallery, the Royal Academy, the Tate Gallery, the Tate Modern, the British Museum, the Victoria and Albert Museum, and the Science Museum. There are many other fascinating museums in and around London, one idiosyncratic example being Madame Tussaud's, with its collection of waxworks of famous people.

London's theaters are legendary. There are more than forty, from the Royal Opera House to the London Palladium. Visitors should plan well ahead to see the choice available, and book in advance whenever possible.

Beyond London, there is a wealth of heritage, arts, and history to discover in the main metropolitan centers and regions of England, including one of the new "wonders of the natural world," the Eden Project, in Cornwall. Information is available through the regional tourist boards.

Some Formal Occasions and What to Wear

Ascot is famous as a horse-racing event, but it is perhaps even more famous for the fact that it is a notable society fashion occasion, at which women show off their clothes, especially their hats. It attracts wide media interest. On the other hand, the traditional Englishman watching the national summer sport of cricket at Lord's cricket ground in London, the home of the game, will wear the exclusive club tie of the home club, the Marylebone Cricket Club (MCC), together with a Panama hat, and even a blue blazer, regardless of how hot it is. Equally, if you are attending the Royal Regatta at Henley, particularly if you are a member of the very exclusive Leander Rowing Club, dress protocol demands that you wear an appropriate shirt and tie.

"Cool Britannia"

In recent times, British fashion designers have gained increasing prominence in the world of *haute couture*. This has led to a resurgence of the notion of "cool Britannia" across society, which in turn has forced change on many major chains and suppliers in the clothes industry who were losing contact with their public. For example, at the end of the 1990s Marks & Spencer had to reinvent themselves by employing some top names in fashion to "rethink" their product lines (including their famous "St. Michael" brand of lingerie!).

Fashion, of course, is very much part of "lifestyle," and has quickly fed into contemporary expectations of behavior and etiquette, for example, in eating out. Apart from notable exceptions in London such as the Ritz Hotel, and the traditional gentlemen's clubs of Pall Mall, St. James's, and Piccadilly, smart casual wear (not a suit and tie, except for business lunches/dinners) when eating out is now the norm.

Inevitably, this new, "no rules," supposedly relaxed dress code in public leads to widespread variations in interpretation. "Smart casual" for one man could mean a patterned T-shirt, jeans, and sneakers; for another it could mean a polo-necked sweater with black trousers and leather shoes.

"CASUAL" IS GOOD

"Casual," which projects the idea of being relaxed and at ease, is the new chic in today's society. By definition, such an attitude challenges the formal behavior of earlier generations, which was characterized by the notion of the "stiff upper lip," of not giving into one's emotions in the face of difficulties. The royal family has also embraced a "casual" approach in recent years—particularly well demonstrated by the highly successful Pop Concert held in the garden of Buckingham Palace in the summer of 2002 to mark the Queen's Golden Jubilee. Who would have thought it possible that the program would open with Brian May, lead guitarist of the 1970s pop group Queen, standing on top of the palace roof playing his own version of the national anthem, "God Save the Queen"?

SHOPPING

Shopping is, of course, both a chore and a pleasure, depending on what you are buying. In towns and cities, supermarkets of all sizes generally supply the week's basic food needs, and there are smaller, specialist shops of all kinds. (Note that a "chemist"—an unfamiliar term to many visitors—sells drugs and medicines, along with all kinds of toiletries and perfumes.) Many villages still have their own "village shop," or general store, that sells a huge variety of goods and often doubles as a post office. Markets for fresh food and other items regularly take place in many towns. These traditionally offer good value.

For other needs, the larger towns and cities have department stores, small boutiques for clothes, and all the usual "high-street" suppliers. Many of London's world-famous stores, such as those in Knightsbridge, Piccadilly, and Bond Street, are magnets for style-conscious shoppers.

As for souvenirs from Britain, there are many specialties, from fine woven woolen goods from Scotland and Wales down to sweet treats such as Scottish shortbread and Edinburgh rock, fudge and toffee, and, of course, marmalade.

"By Royal Appointment"

Official suppliers of goods and services to the royal family receive a special kind of patronage. They can apply for a royal warrant permitting them to display a sign that they are "By Royal Appointment . . ." for example, " . . . suppliers of provisions and household goods to Her Majesty the Queen" or " . . . outfitters and saddlers to HRH The Prince of Wales." Find this on a jam jar, and you know you are eating well!

It is also interesting to seek out the old and unusual, and in all the cities and in countless country towns you can spend hours browsing for anything from antique silver, furniture, and paintings to secondhand books and "junk." Britain seems to have an almost endless supply of such items, from quaint and quirky, through attractive and affordable, to unique and costing a fortune. Many towns also have regular antiques fairs and flea markets, which often offer real bargains and are well worth a visit.

SPORTING LIFE

Though not for generations masters of so many of the sports they invented—including cricket, tennis, and football (with the honorable exception of rugby)—the British are obsessed with the sporting life. The homage paid at the altars of the sporting gods is almost without precedent. Principal amongst such "gods," of course, is the phenomenon of David Beckham, even though in the summer of 2003 he left Manchester United to play for Real Madrid.

Football

Football (soccer), above all, has even been described as the "new religion," driven by the multimillion-pound clubs of the Premier Division, dominated in recent times by Manchester United, Arsenal, Newcastle United, Chelsea, and Liverpool. It is a huge industry in its own right with all the above clubs (as well as others) listed on the London Stock Exchange.

Thankfully now mostly free of the hooligan element (at least in routine home matches) and mob violence, the traditional working-class interest in football has given way to a complete cross-cultural involvement, with greater numbers of women and families watching the games than ever before. The same applies to rugby football, whether League or Union (the latter until recent years being played by nonprofessionals, and which always claims to be the true game).

"Being a good loser" is most noticeably (but not exclusively) linked to English middle-class culture, which applauds everyone for taking part, even if the game ends in defeat. In other words, winning is not necessarily the main point. This emphasis on the value of joining in, or taking part, reinforced through schools, especially the private schools, goes back for generations. In some ways, it is akin to the community spirit that is seen in times of war or disaster. It is hardly surprising, therefore, that the so-called "killer instinct" needed to win at sport is rarely developed enough in British players for them to beat the rest of the world.

Cricket

It might be argued that only the quiet, thoughtful persona of the English could have invented a game that can take up to a whole day or, in the case of Test cricket, up to five days, to complete. Self-evidently, it is a serious game, a game of endurance, commitment, and application. Even so, it is actually meant to be fun too. It is fun because everybody in the team takes part either batting or fielding, and usually everybody gets the chance to hit the ball and score runs. Taking part, or "having a go," is very important.

Cricket is also a game demanding fair play by the umpire and players. Put in its simplest form, a very hard ball is hurled (correctly described as "bowled") at the wicket (consisting of three wooden stumps) in front of which, however, a player from the other team is holding a wooden bat. His job is to stop the ball hitting the wicket (and himself), and to score "runs" by hitting the ball as far as possible and running fast (a "run" being the act of running the distance between the wickets at each end of the pitch—the traditional 22 yards (just over 20 meters). The other batsman from the same team, positioned at the other end of the pitch, has to run also, and both must return to positions at the wickets before the ball has been "fielded" and thrown back to the wicket—or they are "out." As noted earlier, in order to make all the right decisions in judging the game, the umpire must be highly experienced, skilled, and fair.

The Horse World

The horse world is big business. On one hand, according to the Pony Club, there are over a million ponies in private hands in Britain, most being for the fun and entertainment of beloved young daughters across the land. Their competitive arenas are the local and national gymkhanas, which test the riding and jumping skills of the youngsters who compete. At the other extreme are the major professional horse-racing events that occur throughout the year.

The biggest event of the calendar is the annual Grand National, which takes place at Aintree, Liverpool, in April. It is a punishing test of endurance for young horses and their riders, both often totally unknown, and which attracts a "one-off" bet on the winner by vast numbers of the population who otherwise would never be seen in a betting shop!

Marathon

There are other important participatory sports enjoyed in England, such as hockey and basketball, but it is marathon walking, especially the grueling 26.2-mile London Marathon, which has become an annual national event—a perfect vehicle for the English idiosyncratic collective character. (There is also the Newcastle-upon-Tyne Half Marathon). It is done in the name of charity—the British always like to support a good cause—and allows vast numbers of ordinary people to contribute, to achieve something (checking one's time is important and hoping to do better next year), and to have fun—some by just walking in outrageous costumes.

Golf

Of all the "leisure" sports, other than walking— which is a traditional pastime, and well organized throughout the country by the Ramblers Association, which ensures that the public has access to the widest possible number of countryside walks—golf attracts the greatest number of participants. For many enthusiasts it has almost become a way of life. As a sport, it is so big that Britain now boasts 2,500 golf courses that welcome visiting golfers— and no self-respecting developer in Spain or Portugal would dream of investing in a new holiday resort designed to attract British vacationers without including at least one golf course in his plans.

THE SEASON

In times gone by, the English "Season," as it is known, was the preserve of the upper classes, who would attend the top sporting and cultural events.

These, and private balls and parties, presented an opportunity for showing off their eligible sons and (particularly) daughters, chiefly in order to find them suitable spouses, as well as showing themselves and keeping up to date with the latest gossip. This is still the case, of course, but socially speaking its relevance is diluted as "new money" mixes with old. Today the Season owes its survival to the members of "corporate Britain," who use the main events as opportunities for promotion.

Main Events

The key sporting events of the year are the Boat Race between Oxford and Cambridge on the Thames (March); the Horse Trials at Badminton (May); Derby Day at Epsom (June); racing at Royal Ascot (July); tennis at Wimbledon (June–July); rowing at Henley (July), and sailing at Cowes, on the Isle of Wight (August).

The cultural events include the Chelsea Flower Show (May); the Royal Academy's Summer Exhibition; and the opera at Glyndebourne in East Sussex (May–September). The last night of the Promenade Concerts, held at the Albert Hall, London, each year, otherwise known as the "Proms," is also considered part of the fun, because it presents an entirely laudable opportunity for displaying good-natured patriotism by waving the Union Jack (Flag) and singing "Land of Hope and Glory" with great gusto at the end of the proceedings.

Naturally, if you go to any or all of these events you gain points for wearing the most fashionable clothes; you would consequently never go alone, but always with a group of friends or family, and would expect to see and be seen by a great many other friends and acquaintances.

PUBLIC HOLIDAYS
New Year's Day (January 1)
Good Friday (two days before Easter)
Easter Monday (the day after Easter)
Early Spring Holiday (first Monday in May)
Spring Holiday (last Monday in May)
Late Summer Holiday (last Monday in August)
Christmas Day (December 25)
Boxing Day (December 26)

DIY AND GARDENING

The weekend is the time when DIY ("Do It Yourself") and gardening enthusiasts change into their alter egos of craftsmen and begin or continue the process of transforming their homes. This is an extension of the "Englishman's home is his castle" syndrome, and is a wonderful manifestation of an individual's sense of identity and singularity, as well as a source of well-being. Given the fact that home ownership in Britain (in England approximately 70 percent) is the highest in Europe, it is not difficult to understand why these industries, led by nationwide chains of hardware supermarkets, and given a further boost by TV makeover programs, are so enormous.

The quintessentially English pastime of gardening is enjoyed by men and women, young and old, through all the seasons. A garden epitomizes the English nostalgia for the country way of life, and for Blake's "green and pleasant land." The annual amount of money spent on garden-related products throughout the country is considerably greater than that spent on DIY. Gardening books, magazines, and programs on radio and TV are a major part of Britain's culture.

Britain is full of wonderful stately homes, parks and gardens, in both public and private ownership, that are open to visitors.

TRAVEL AND TRANSPORT

If you are driving, remember that in Britain you drive on the left! Roads are generally good, with a network of motorways (expressways), designated by an M, for example M1, M2 and so on, and lesser A and B roads, which are usually the more scenic routes for those who wish to see some countryside. Some rural roads are little more than narrow, winding tracks. The national speed limits are 70 mph on motorways, 60 mph on open roads, and 30 mph in any "built-up," area, that is, wherever there are buildings. Be careful to watch your speeds.

Britain has a reasonable public transportation system. Everybody complains about it, but most forms of transportation generally run as scheduled. Trains are the fastest, of course, but the cheapest form of long-distance travel is by bus (coach). Nationwide scheduled coach services are run by National Express, and there are many other bus services operating around the country.

When traveling around Britain, it is a good idea to go to the local tourist information offices. They can help with accommodation, travel advice, and suggestions for what to see and do in the area.

chapter seven

FRIENDSHIP, FAMILY, & SOCIAL LIFE

INFORMALITY AND FRIENDSHIP

A view long held by many foreigners is that it takes time to make friends with the English, but that then it becomes something significant and permanent. This may still be true. Today's drive for cheerful informality, with the common use of first names in a great many areas of everyday life, especially the world of work, may give a different impression. It is based on the assumption that such informality makes everyone feel more comfortable and relaxed—but it does not necessarily equate with friendship and the desire to spend more time together outside the working environment. The best advice is not to push or assume too much.

This same principle holds true of neighbors ("the higher the fence, the better the neighbor"). On other occasions when people are brought together, for whatever reasons, such as when supporting local volunteer organizations, the English "reserve" tends to be very noticeable. People are happy to give up their time but not their privacy. Sometimes, this is seen as cold, or as bad manners; but it is probably simply politeness.

Understanding "Politeness"

The English form of politeness is sometimes misunderstood. Being polite in a formal context, such as in an office, may involve joining in and appearing to have a good time at a big social event organized by your company, or at a private dinner arranged by one of the directors. This is considered good manners; but for many English people, that's all it is. Likewise, if two strangers strike up a friendly conversation on a train, for example, this is usually purely good manners, and the relationship is unlikely to develop further.

Such occasions can, of course, be the beginning of a real friendship, but don't be hurt or surprised if the relationship stops there.

Greeting, Kissing, and Touching

The usual formal greeting is a "How do you do?" (or, less formally, "Hello") and a firm handshake, but with a lighter touch between men and women. A limp handshake from a man is considered insincere, effeminate, untrustworthy, or sloppy, or all four.

On social occasions, say at a dinner party involving colleagues and their partners, handshakes between men and women give way to "social kissing," whereby the man lightly holds the woman by the upper arms and barely kisses the woman's cheeks, while the woman "kisses the air," making a soft (pretend kissing) "mmuh" sound. Increasingly, both cheeks are kissed. Close friends would exchange hugs and contact kisses.

Although, historically, the English are quite restrained and composed, dislike exhibitionism in their contact with others, and abhor "space invaders"—those who move too close during a conversation—hugging is now more prevalent, not least among the younger generation.

Within the family today, men play an increasing part in the traditional "mothering" role. The old situation of physical contact between father and son being restricted to a handshake—a formal standard of behavior that is still expected in certain contexts—is gradually giving way to a warmer physical relationship.

MANNERS—FORMAL AND INFORMAL

Many British people admire the widespread use of the term "Sir" as a mark of respect in America, both inside and outside the classroom, including the home. In Britain the use of the term is waning in ordinary everyday life. It continues in schools—especially in public schools, where it is perceived as an essential courtesy in a more respectful and disciplined environment—and, of course, in the Armed Services.

Today young people in Britain show less deference to their elders, are generally much more relaxed about relationships, and take a more egalitarian, "laidback" view of society as a whole, and their place within it.

Terms of Endearment

The visitor to Britain is sometimes astonished to be addressed in rather intimate terms. In southern England, on the buses and in the shops, you may very well be addressed as "love," "lovey," "dear," "darling," "pet," or "petal"—and perhaps, if you are lucky, "my lover" in Devon. As you go north you will hear different terms, such as "chuck" (around Liverpool and the northwest), "duck" (around Sheffield and the northwest), and "hen" (in Scotland). As a market trader weighs up some apples for you, he might say, "Just over a kilo. All right, darlin'?" Don't be alarmed! These are all gentle terms of address, never intended to be overfamiliar or to offend.

"Thank You" and "Sorry!"

The British are strong on polite language. You will hear "Please," "Thank you," and "Sorry!"

everywhere. Any service, however small, requires a "Thank you"—whatever you have just bought or paid for, whether it is a bus ticket, a trolleyful of groceries, a tankful of gas, or even a charity sticker when you have put some money in a donation box. And that is the end of it; the other person does not reply, as in the U.S.A., "You're welcome," though they may say "Thank you" back, as a way of finishing off the conversation. The British say, "Thank you" when somebody pays them a compliment of any kind, they say, "Thank you, how kind of you!" when somebody helps them with something. People on the radio or TV say, "Thank you" to the interviewer, presumably for the opportunity to give their opinion. The British are indeed a grateful lot!

"Sorry" may be "the hardest word" for Elton John, but, in fact, it is one of the most widely used words among the British. Is this an example of British ultra-politeness, or just plain good manners? The British say, "Sorry!" almost involuntarily as an apology for any possible inconvenience or interruption for which he or she might feel responsible. They say, "Sorry!" or even "So sorry!" if they brush past somebody in the street, or touch somebody accidentally—invading somebody's private space. They may even say "Sorry" if somebody else treads on their toe (because their toe got in the way)! They say,

"Sorry?" to signal the fact that they have not heard what someone has said, and to request repetition. ("Excuse me" is not normally used in any of these contexts, as it is in the U.S.A.—it is used to attract someone's attention, or in politely, or sometimes less politely, asking the person addressed to move aside.)

They will say, "I'm very sorry," or "I'm so sorry," as a sympathetic lead-in when giving some bad news, or when causing inconvenience or discomfort, such as when a doctor has to make a painful investigation. Even a traffic warden, when sticking a traffic violation notice on your car, may say, "Sorry, I'm only doing my job."

THE NEW FAMILIARITY

On Fridays, as one leaves work, it is a common courtesy to say to one's colleagues, "Have a good weekend." Another expression, "Have a nice day," learned from America, or the English version, "Have a good day," is now heard more often, not just from friends and colleagues, but from those at supermarket checkouts, and serving in shops and restaurants. This has been adopted as part of the informal friendliness of modern youth culture, along with another trend—the frequent use of customers' first names in day-to-day business dealings. Such familiarity is new to the traditionally reserved English, and often mildly irritates the older generations, who feel that such manners are presumptuous.

For the visitor, it is better to play safe and not address elderly people by their first names, unless invited to do so!

THE FAMILY

Children

An old saying, "Children should be seen and not heard," is alive and well in Britain, and applies in the main to public places, such as restaurants—which are not all particularly "child-friendly." The feeling is simply that children should be reasonably well-behaved, and should not annoy other people by making an excessive noise or running around in an unruly way. People are generally tolerant and kindly with children, but parents are expected to check their behavior.

Today British children are encouraged to speak their mind at a much earlier age, and tend to be much more articulate than previous generations. They may be spending hours each day on their computers playing games or researching for their homework, but today's youngsters are generally better informed and more engaged than their parents were at the same age, and are encouraged to think about topical issues.

Many British children today live in a world of designer clothes, mobile phones, partying, and a media that addresses their every need (and whenever possible creates new "needs"). Like their counterparts throughout the industrialized world, they have more disposable income ("pocket money") than ever before.

At sixteen children can go into pubs on their own (and be served nonalcoholic drinks); they can legally have sexual intercourse, and marry with permission. At eighteen, they can vote, purchase alcohol and tobacco, and join the Armed Services.

Family Meals

It is often regretted that today families rarely sit and eat meals together in the traditional way. It seems to be the case that in many families this is now limited to Sunday lunch or supper. With both parents working and children participating in after-school activities such as music lessons, or drama or sports clubs, meals in the working week tend to be *ad hoc*, to suit the various comings and goings. The evening meal will often be something quick and easy—such as a dish bought ready-made and heated in a microwave oven, pasta, "something out of a can," or a pizza delivered to the door.

Visitors will notice that a significant number of permanent relationships these days (including younger family units) involve unmarried couples who refer to each other as their "partner" rather than their husband or wife.

Nannies

The children of the old aristocratic and upper-class families always had a nanny in attendance—a woman living in her own quarters in the house, who had complete care of them. She would sometimes stay for the rest of her life, looking after successive generations of children, and being regarded with great affection by the family.

Special training colleges, known for their high standards, were set up for "nursery nurses"; those nannies left with good qualifications and could expect the best jobs, with excellent pay and living conditions.

Demand for nannies grew in the economic "boom" years of the 1990s, mostly in cases where both father and mother had busy and well-paid professional careers. "Nannying," trained or untrained, became quite a popular job for young women, and many went to work in other countries, becoming one of Britain's successful cultural exports. In harder times, nannies may be dispensed with.

Pets

The British preoccupation with pets is an indisputable fact of life. In 2002 Britain was estimated to have 7.5 million cats, and just over six million dogs (dogs used to outnumber cats), with rabbits in third place at just over one million. Keeping goldfish and tropical fish is also a thriving and growing hobby.

If there is a dog in a house that you are visiting, the important thing for you to realize is that it may well be a situation of "love me, love my dog." In this case, the owner thinks the world of the dog, and does not believe that any sensible person can think otherwise—even though you might find it intensely intrusive, annoying, and possibly even smelly!

Unfortunately many people underestimate the amount of time, money, and energy needed to look after pets, particularly, dogs. Every year before Christmas, there is a plea from animal care institutions and charities, such as the RSPCA (Royal Society for the Prevention of Cruelty to Animals), to think very carefully about buying a pet as a present. "A dog is not just for Christmas; it is for life" is the message. But thousands of unwanted dogs end up on the streets and in temporary care homes like the Battersea Dogs' Home in London, which in 2002 cared for some 12,500 cats and dogs, with 2,900 stray dogs returned to their owners.

Pet Travel Scheme

The Pet Travel Scheme, launched by the British Government in 2000, allows pet cats and dogs from twenty-four Western European countries, and twenty-six "long-haul" countries, including Australia, New Zealand, Singapore, and Japan, to enter or reenter the U.K. without quarantine, provided they meet certain conditions, including vaccination against rabies.

The media frequently feature sentimental animal stories, for example about abandoned donkeys in a European country; and low-budget TV programs show pets doing "clever" or "amusing" things. Pet lovers also make the headlines from time to time when they leave their entire estate to a home for abandoned dogs or cats.

The "animal rights" movement has had considerable impact on government policy; for example, research on live animals is now banned in the cosmetics industry, but is allowed under strict rules for scientific research for the benefit of human welfare.

Gift Giving
As suggested earlier, when visiting someone's home for a meal it is customary to bring flowers, chocolates, or a bottle of wine. Visitors coming to stay from overseas would do well to bring a gift for the parents and, perhaps, appropriate little presents typical of their own hometown or region for the children.

Gift giving in a more general sense, as for example in bringing presents for friends and family from exotic lands, is commonplace. Christmas (for most British people—not only the Christians) and birthdays are occasions for presents and parties. Younger people tend to be very spontaneous with regard to gift giving and, among friends, tend to exchange presents and cards for birthdays and other occasions much more readily than their parents do.

THE CLASS SYSTEM
The following description is very generalized, and barely begins to cover all the many details and nuances of that very English phenomenon, "class." It is true to say, however, that the most telling

indicators of an English person's class are his or her accent and behavior—in this matter the English can generally sum each other up within moments of meeting.

In practice, class is no longer a barrier to either casual social mixing or genuine friendship; but people often feel more comfortable associating with others from the same background. A working-class person might feel uncomfortable at a "society" wedding, for example, as might an aristocrat in a certain kind of pub, but this is a generalization, and a certain amount of self-confidence would carry the day for both.

The Upper Class
The upper class generally refers to the aristocracy and its offshoots, and was traditionally the "ruling class," although this is no longer absolutely the case in today's fluid social mix. It largely consists of people with inherited wealth, and includes some of the oldest families in the land, many of them titled. Along with land, wealth, titles, and privileges came certain obligations and responsibilities; not the least of these was the duty to behave as befitted

one's rank. This is still the case among those who are genuinely "upper class"—good manners are of the utmost importance.

The upper class generally manages to keep itself to itself, minding its own business at all times. Many marriages continue to be "arranged" by a process of carefully managed introductions. Those who find themselves short of cash open their houses (the "stately homes of England," as they were famously described by Noel Coward) to the public and charge a fee for entry, or live in impoverished circumstances among some remaining priceless antiques.

Members of the upper class often have a distinctive, mannered accent, which is delivered in a very precise manner. A more slowly delivered version of this is known as "an upper-class drawl." Increasingly, however, the younger generation is inclined to avoid such mannerisms of speech in order *not* to appear upper class!

The upper class is defined first and foremost by the families that belong to it. To be from one of the "old" families is virtually a prerequisite of being upper class. Other pointers are education (at good private schools such as Eton or Harrow, followed by university—Oxford or Cambridge); wealth (often, these days, in the form of land or property rather than cash); and, to a certain extent, occupation and pastimes, which include the traditional country sports of hunting, shooting, and fishing. Many upper-class people keep horses, and ride for pleasure (which often includes fox-hunting) and competitively (including show jumping), as well as taking an interest in racing.

Those who are interested to know "who's who" in the aristocracy can consult *Burke's Peerage*, which gives the pedigrees of titled families.

Fox-Hunting

Over a hundred years ago, the playwright and satirist Oscar Wilde described fox-hunting as "the unspeakable in pursuit of the uneatable." Today, it has become a social and political battleground.

Those opposed to the sport do so on the grounds of cruelty to animals, and it has become a major issue in Parliament, with the Labour government committed to abolishing it. In other words, it is not so much a campaign to save the fox as a trophy in the battle between "rich" and "poor."

The Middle Class

There has always been a middle class of those whose wealth or occupations put them somewhere between the aristocracy and the peasants. Landowners and professional people—"gentlemen"—were later joined by those who made money during or after the Industrial Revolution. The middle class is broadly based, and even divides itself into lower-middle and upper-middle class, according to wealth, level of education, and perceived standing within the community. This refinement of class distinction could be invented only by a society obsessed with status and the pursuit of minutiae.

The middle class these days encompasses the professional, managerial, and so-called "upwardly mobile" sections of society (as well, perhaps, as a "downwardly mobile" section from the upper class), and is seen to represent the greater part of the population as a whole, certainly in the southern half of England. It is generally less rigid in its behavior and in matters of etiquette than the upper class.

Middle-class values formed the backbone of society and provided the skilled professionals and administrators who ran the Empire. Education is important for the middle classes, at a private or good state school, preferably followed by university. Pastimes are not so well defined, but sports that call for expensive equipment, special clothing, or extensive training and practice, such as golf and tennis, are regarded as a middle-class preserve.

Although they tend to approach life in a more relaxed way, like the upper class, the middle classes also enjoy establishment pomp and circumstance, such as the Opening of Parliament by the Queen, or the pageantry associated with Royal jubilees. Formal social occasions, such as a wedding or a ball for a daughter who is "coming out," that is, making her formal debut in society, are held in great style. Once an upper-class tradition, launching one's daughter in society in this way, in the hope that she will find a suitable husband, has now been taken up by the "new rich." The custom is encouraged by such publications as *The Tatler*, which features these debutantes and their parties in its pages.

The Working Class

"Working-class Britain" is a phrase still used by socialists and trade unionists. It was coined in the context of the exploitation and social inequality that resulted from the rise of nineteenth-century capitalism. Its use today continues to reinforce the historic class divisions of Britain, and of England in particular.

Labour governments are always reminded that the Labour Party was founded by the trade union movement at the beginning of the twentieth century to champion the needs of its members. For most of its life the Party has been bankrolled through the trade union levy on its members.

The working class has its own rituals and etiquette that inform behavior and determine what is expected of its members. Working-class culture is projected and played out every week through the TV "soaps," principally *Coronation Street* (the longest-running), which reflects the way of life in the northeast of England, and *Eastenders*, which reflects life in and around London's East End. These soaps, of course, attract viewers from across the cultural spectrum.

Like the soaps, working-class life has traditionally revolved around the local pub, working men's clubs (women were, traditionally, never admitted, but political correctness has forced changes in recent times), soccer (known as football)—with at times almost tribal loyalty—betting shops, bingo halls, and brass bands, especially in the north. In its own way, it is a culture that also breeds its own form of snobbishness, which would quickly find fault with anyone who was thought to be stepping out of line, such as showing aspirations to rise "above his station," or class.

For example, there could be consequences within the community if somebody were seen joining the local fox hunt (which is considered upper class) or a smart local health clinic (which is seen as middle class) or supporting Rugby

Union (which is seen as middle class) instead of Rugby League (which is seen as working class.) And you definitely wouldn't dare think of ordering anything but beer (or a soft drink) in a working men's club—never wine!

"Knowing One's Place"

A comic TV sketch of the 1970s perfectly sums up English attitudes to class. It features three men of different heights, dress, and headgear, standing in a row. The tallest and best-dressed of the three glances at the other two and says, "I look down on both of them." The man in the middle, dressed in an ordinary suit, turns to the tall man and says, "I look up to him"; then to the small man, dressed in working clothes with a cloth cap, and says, "but I look down on him." Finally, the smallest man just says, "I know my place." This sketch may seem an anachronism today, but the fact remains that class divisions are recognized, even if not discussed.

The "Chattering Classes"

There is a new cross-section of society, drawn from all classes, known as the "Chattering Classes." It consists of people involved in the media, whose business it is to tell the rest of the country what to think and why—from writers and journalists in the printed media, to those on TV and radio, together with academics, actors (increasingly these days), and those who inhabit the world of the Arts generally. Many of them are also politicians.

One of their characteristics is that they take themselves, and their mission of setting the social and cultural agenda, very seriously. As a group they tend to allow themselves to be ruder than other people, because of their view of their own importance.

But, like politicians, they live a life somewhat apart, and are usually greeted with a healthy skepticism by the rest of society. They are also the promoters of what is increasingly regarded as a modern social bugbear, "political correctness"—the proscribed barriers to the use of language or behavior that could be perceived as offensive to any one (minority) group. Thus, we now have "chairperson," or even "chair," instead of the generic chairman, and a "chalkboard" instead of a blackboard in the classroom.

The chattering classes give lively parties, and are stimulating company.

The "*Nouveaux Riches*"
This is a disparaging term, but the class is as old as history. It specifically refers to those who make an ostentatious display of newly acquired wealth.

It can include the self-made man, who from humble beginnings has accumulated a great deal of money, probably from trade, or the suddenly rich millionaire, such as a lottery winner. Such a person might for example buy an unnecessarily large and luxurious house or car—which is seen as vulgar or tasteless—or start throwing huge and extravagant parties.

In today's social environment many of the traditional self-made people, whether industrialists or tradesmen, also tend to receive a public "honour" as well. Those modest people who do not make a great display of their new wealth are treated with due respect and would not be described as "*nouveau riche.*"

Read the Books!
The writer and lawyer John Mortimer, creator of *Rumpole of the Bailey*—a richly comic observation of English customs and moral attitudes as seen through the eyes of an old-fashioned barrister (advocate)—once remarked that the basis of all English literature is class—moving from Chaucer, through Shakespeare, through Trollope, to the present day. Read almost any piece of fiction by an English author, and it will give you further insight into the manners and mores of the English.

"Lifestyle," not "Class"

Finally, what is increasingly being called "lifestyle" could well be the next paradigm in the shifting notions of class. Driven by "Yuppies" ("young, upwardly mobile professional people") and "Dinks" (couples with "dual incomes, no kids"), and reinforced by a growing media fixation on youth culture, the lifestyle gurus preach a gospel of instant access to a quality of life determined not by wealth, education, moral values, or merit, but by the fashion of the moment—the color you paint your bedroom, the positioning of your furniture (*feng shui*), and the designer clothes you wear. The followers of "lifestyle" may well see themselves as the new social leaders!

TABOO SUBJECTS

In the context of polite conversation, the traditional social taboos used to be politics, sex, and religion. To this might be added the subject of money. These subjects were all considered likely to raise tempers or cause embarrassment, and thus disturb the atmosphere at the dinner table. Today some things have changed, but vestiges of the old feelings persist, and visitors should be careful before saying anything that might cause offense or embarrassment. Religion is not a subject for discussion if you are unsure of your company.

Money

The subject of money—in the sense of how much or how little one has—is not for general discussion, being thought too personal. Also, even in today's world of the National Lottery and the TV game show *Who Wants to be a Millionaire?*, there are still English people who think that there is something rather vulgar or disreputable about being in "trade." In other words, the perception of a darker side to the processes of making money continues to lurk in the nation's subconscious.

On the other hand, it is perfectly acceptable to talk about how you have managed to save in small ways—such as finding a bottle of good wine for half price in a supermarket!

The British upper classes are deeply suspicious of conspicuous consumption, or "showing off"; but this generalization is often stood on its head by the increasing numbers of newly rich, many of whom are very enthusiastic about displaying their wealth. In Britain demonstrable wealth is not necessarily the measure of success. People are admired because, as in sport, they took part— they had a go. Perhaps they failed; but they will be admired more for who they are (essentially as a person, although it may include status) and how they conduct their lives. It is a fact that someone from the upper classes who finds himself with no

money and no prospects will usually be treated
with more respect than a person with no manners
or "breeding," who is in a similar situation. In the
end, dignity, culture, and status are more highly
regarded than the possession of money.

Politics is OK

With the arrival of the televising of Parliament,
and New Labour's so-called "engaging" approach
to the political process, attitudes have softened a
little toward the discussion of politics. Good
manners continue to dictate that the less you say
about your own political convictions the better;
but it is all right to discuss politicians themselves,
including gossip about their private lives.

Other Europeans, on the other hand, are much
more concerned with matters such as bribery and
corruption, and believe that a "public" person's
private life, especially his or her sex life, is their
own business.

Sex is More OK Than It Was

The British seem to have had an odd relationship
with sex for a long time, but are more inclined to
talk openly about it today, at least in a general
way. One's own sex life, however, is as private as
you wish.

Attitudes toward sexuality have never been
straightforward historically. This ambivalence has

sometimes generated extreme outcomes—from periods of repression, as in the Puritan Commonwealth of Oliver Cromwell, or the time of Queen Victoria (when some people even covered piano legs out of perverse notions of modesty), to periods of excess as in the Regency period of the early nineteenth century, or indeed, some might say, today.

Sex and sexual repression have been a major preoccupation of British writers, dramatists, artists, entertainers, and social reformers for generations—the long-running farce in London's West End, *No Sex, Please, We're British*, is a classic example of its genre. In the meantime, after the so-called "sexual liberation" of post-1960s Britain, the country has the third-highest divorce rate in the world (mostly initiated by women) and the highest number of single mothers under the age of twenty in Europe. Both written and broadcast media support sexual freedom in terms of choice and orientation, and even preteen magazines promote interest in sex, directly and indirectly.

What Does the Foreign Visitor Do?

Of course, it is difficult for an outsider to know exactly who is who and what should be what in any particular social context in England. The better news, however, is that nothing is expected of a foreigner except to have good manners. A visitor who simply "fits in" is welcomed.

If a visitor from overseas has bad manners, this would not be mentioned, but would simply reinforce the traditional English view that social order and civility cease at the White Cliffs of Dover.

chapter eight

BUSINESS BRIEFING

A BIRD'S-EYE VIEW

The British economy has been one of the great success stories of the Blair administration to date, maintaining low inflation and the lowest interest rates in a generation, achieving annual growth of around 2.5 percent—against a backdrop of a boom in the service and knowledge-based sectors but a depressed manufacturing base—as well as maintaining an independent currency. The battle to join the euro has yet to be fought, and may well be lost when a referendum is called. At the same time, the government has levied the largest increases in indirect taxation in a generation to fund an unprecedented increase in spending on public services, especially the National Health Service.

Britain's principal trading partner is the European Union (accounting for over 50 percent of trade in goods and services); once it had been the British Empire. In fact, the loss of Empire with its captive markets has forced British industry and commerce to become far more competitive. A "wake-up" call was first sounded by Margaret Thatcher, but only slowly and to some extent reluctantly has it been implemented. It is ironic that three of the ten most productive car plants in the whole of Europe are in Britain, but are Japanese owned, demonstrating that the British worker can indeed be one of the best, given the right working environment and motivation. The British in fact work longer hours than any other country in Europe, coming fourth in the world, after U.S.A., Japan, and Australia, in the total number of hours worked during the year.

Britain's biggest foreign investor is the United States, and vice versa. This is not surprising, since these countries have a common history, language, and culture. It is important, however, to recognize that there can be significant differences in the perception of history, in the use of language, and in cultural norms and aspirations. This is not the place to examine these issues in detail, but it is useful for American visitors, especially businessmen, to be aware of the fact that such differences do exist.

As islanders, the British are a mercantile race by nature. Trading with the rest of world is a routine part of commercial and industrial daily life, as it has been since long before the days of Empire. In fact, although it has less than one percent of the world's population, Britain is the world's fifth-largest trading nation. This "overseas" trade, as it is called, today accounts for nearly 30 percent of GDP and continues to be a vital component of the national economy.

Britain's principal markets are the U.S.A. (£29 billion; U.S. $46.4 billion), followed by Germany (£22 billion; U.S. $ 35.2 billion), France (£18 billion; U.S. $28.8 billion), the Netherlands (£15 billion; U.S. $24 billion), and the Irish Republic (£12 billion; U.S. $19.2 billion). Japan is tenth (£3.5 billion; U.S. $5.6 billion). Conversely, the main suppliers are almost the same, with the U.S. first (£28.5 billion; U.S. $45.6 billion), followed by Germany (£27.5 billion; U.S. $44 billion), France (£18 billion; U.S. $28.8 billion), the Netherlands (£15 billion; U.S. $24 billion), and Japan (£10 billion; U.S. $16 billion). In tenth position is Hong Kong (£6 billion; U.S. $9.6 billion).

Traditional manufacturing industries, including the "heavy" industries of coal, iron, and steel, like those of the G7 group generally, continue to decline. Nevertheless, specialist machinery and transport equipment accounted for 47 percent of exports and 46 percent of imports in 2000, with aerospace, chemicals, and electronics becoming increasingly significant exports. Fuels, chemicals, beverages, and tobacco continue to make significant contributions, as do services, such as transport, communications, construction, insurance, financial services, computer and information services, and royalties and license fees. GDP growth rate has been around 2 to 2.5 percent and is expected to remain so well into the first decade of the new century.

BUSINESS FORMALITIES

The Handshake
When you first meet businesspeople, and also on leaving, there will be the usual round of firm (but not bone-crunching, and not protracted) handshakes. As yet, the English have not adopted the French habit of routinely shaking hands. Typical greetings are, "Hello; nice to meet you," or the traditional "How do you do?"

Business Cards
The handshake is generally, but not always, followed by the exchange of business cards. Cards for the professional classes, including civil servants, are usually discreet, simple designs with black ink on a white background. For those involved in, say, manufacturing, marketing, or public relations, they are more colorful and include the company logo. Unlike the Japanese, the British tend simply to glance at the card without studying it, pocket it, and reciprocate with one of their own, if they have one.

The Value of Good Manners

The British believe that "manners makyth man" and are good for business too. Quiet courtesy will make a very positive impression on your host. Show a degree of reticence and deference, and remember to say, "please," "thank you," and so on.

First Names

Take the lead from your host regarding the use of first names; as a general rule it is best to take things gradually. Age differences are also a determinant. As noted earlier, younger people (and the young at heart!) are more inclined to use first names, American-style, but you need to be sure of your ground before assuming this is the level of communication preferred by your host. It is a fact, too, of course, that the wide use of e-mail has had a significant impact on communications; the American protocol of "Hi, Peter" is widespread, but English traditionalists often prefer the conventional letter-writing format, using "Dear Peter."

Friendship, and Being Friendly

Bear in mind that the British tend to compartmentalize their lives and have a heightened sense of privacy and personal space.

This is reinforced by adherence to the old axiom of "never mix business and pleasure"—hence a reticence to "make friends" in business, in the sense of close relationships. People are often aware of the possibility of spoiling a good working relationship by making presumptions of something closer. For many of the younger generation this is no longer the barrier it once was. However, there is a world of difference between being friendly toward someone and assuming that this is real friendship.

WRITTEN COMMUNICATIONS

The forms of address that include the terms "Mr.," "Mrs.," "Miss," or "Ms.") continue to be used, and are probably still considered the "normal" mode. However, the practice is growing of writing simply "John Smith," "Jane Smith," or even "J. Smith."

Recognition of an individual's professional status, such as Dr. (medical or academic doctor) or Professor, or rank within the Armed Services, etc., continues to be required etiquette. Many people, particularly in private correspondence, continue to use the traditional form of address to a gentleman, "Esquire," as in "John Smith, Esq.," but that practice is very likely to disappear within the next generation.

FORMAL MEETINGS AND DRESS CODE

The days of the rolled umbrella, dark suit, and bowler hat have practically disappeared—with the occasional exception in the City of London. On the other hand, regardless of some relaxation of dress codes in certain contexts (see below), smart dressing for business meetings is essential. This means dark suits for men, and a neat dark skirt or trousers and jacket for women. Personal hygiene and a well-groomed appearance are important. There is widespread use of fragrance these days for both men and women; subtlety is still your best friend in this department.

Foreign visitors who wish to wear the traditional attire of their native cultures, particularly at a formal business reception, would be warmly welcomed.

"Dressing Down"

In the 1990s and into the new century, various large and small companies acceded to the requests of staff to create a more relaxed atmosphere on Fridays, the end of the working week, by what has been called "dressing down," that is, by coming to work in smart but casual clothes, and not wearing a conventional shirt and tie. This concession most benefited the male workforce, given that women had for some time been wearing the kind of fashionable clothing that could hardly have been imagined a generation before.

Men's Lib

In 2003 a male worker in the back office (that is, not dealing with the public) of a government agency won a case of discrimination against his employer, which had insisted that he wear a suit and tie to work at all times.

PUNCTUALITY AND OFFICE LIFE

Being on time for appointments is essential in a business context. Don't be late. On the other hand, don't arrive too early (other than a few minutes at most). This rule also holds for evening arrangements, for example where you are expected for dinner at a restaurant. If you are unavoidably held up, telephone.

An exchange of pleasantries is expected at the start of a meeting; but avoid excessive loudness, trying too hard to be humorous, being over-familiar, or even being excessively polite with those above you.

Entertainment

With an eye on costs and the pressures of time, extended business lunches are rare these days; increasingly, employees take a short lunch break, often going for a quick walk and bringing back a sandwich to eat in the office.

If you are invited to a business lunch (usually

taken from 12:30 p.m. onward) you should assume that you will be back in the office by around 2:30 p.m. Evening entertainment is not particularly common, except when there is an occasion such as a trade fair or conference.

Smoking in Offices/Public Places

Smoking is now excluded in all public venues, especially on public transportation, in theaters and cinemas, and in increasing numbers of restaurants (although many of the latter offer separate "smoking" and "nonsmoking" areas). Smoking in offices, notably in the larger corporations, is virtually universally excluded, with some companies offering smoking-room facilities. Smoking in pubs, however, is still the norm. Where pubs have restaurant facilities, "no smoking" areas are often available. Around 30 percent of the adult population in Britain smoke.

Gift Giving

Exchanging lavish gifts is not usually expected or done in a British business context. The British are generally not at ease with this aspect of business practice elsewhere in the world, and struggle with the process when formalities require it at home. They are embarrassed if they receive a generous gift, and even more embarrassed if they have to give one. Whether this has to do with a perception that gifts contain an element of bribery, or is simply a manifestation of traditional English shyness and reticence, is debatable. It may also be that in a business relationship a gift seems too personal.

To help the process along, there has been a huge growth in the corporate gift market—"sanitized" gifts with the company logo on them, from umbrellas to ballpoint pens. But this is all done in the cause of good marketing and public relations.

For the visitor bringing gifts, remember they will not necessarily be reciprocated. But don't let this deter you! A present of food or wine or craftwork from your country will always be welcomed.

BUSINESSPEOPLE

The hard realities of doing business in the twenty-first century leave little room for those who used to fine-tune class differences when it came to a choice of employees. Automatic access to the world of work via the "old school tie" has gone, although making useful contacts ("networking") is important. Survival in today's competitive environment has forced management everywhere to become tougher and employ people for their efficiency, multitasking capabilities, and capacity to contribute to the organization in a direct and positive way—not for their looks, social connections, or cultured voice. A new meritocracy has evolved, as well as greater transparency in the way companies operate, especially in the post-Enron environment.

Accountants now tend to be at the center of decision-making, and the considerable tightening of financial rules and regulations, including anti-discriminatory laws (notably sexual and racial discrimination), require increasing transparency in the way business is conducted.

Small- and medium-sized companies account for some 96 percent of all British enterprises. Not surprisingly, among these there are many traditional and family firms—making cheese, shirts, concert pianos, and so on.

These firms are part of the fast-disappearing "skilled craftsmen" foundations that have been at the heart of British entrepreneurial culture for a century and more. Even basic domestic tradesmen, such as plumbers, electricians, and carpenters are increasingly hard to find, partly because the old apprenticeship system was abandoned a generation ago (although the government has made some recent efforts to encourage a simpler version of it), and partly because government attempts at social engineering within the school system have not encouraged trade-orientated syllabuses.

Women in Business

Equal rights for women in the world of work are enshrined in law; but there are areas where the "glass ceiling" continues to inhibit women's advancement. Nevertheless, there are today more women at the top than ever before. Also, the government benefits system is more generous to women, particularly single and working mothers, than ever before.

Despite this, outside the office, such as at trade fairs, conferences, or seminars, many men are still inclined to assume that the women present are probably personal assistants or support staff, so as a woman you would do well to make your executive/managerial position clear at the earliest opportunity—obviously in as subtle and gracious a manner as possible.

NEGOTIATION STYLES

In Britain negotiation and interview styles are markedly different from those in the United States. The British business interview and negotiating style tends to be deferential, indirect, affable, and relaxed, where humor is not necessarily out of place. The American style tends to be shorter and much more direct, where individuals sell themselves hard, leaving the other side in no doubt regarding their strengths and merits. Pleasantries are typically not exchanged.

Remember, too, in this context, that given the typical English inclination toward self-effacement and understatement, you may have to exercise great patience in doing business at this level. If it is generally true that Americans like to be "sold" something, it is equally true that the English generally like to "buy" something, and they can sometimes take an inordinate amount of time to make up their minds. So do not expect a hard sell in Britain. Everything will be understated, and you may well have to probe and even pester in order to determine the real value of the product or service that interests you. In other words, you will actually need to ask!

TRADE UNIONISM

The reform of trade unionism in the Thatcher years helped to bring about the rebirth of the British economy in the mid 1980s. The prosperity that followed has continued more or less uninterrupted ever since—apart from one or two unhappy glitches, especially Britain's sudden withdrawal in 1991 from the European Monetary Union (EMU), which caused huge increases in interest rates, resulting in many people losing their homes, and businesses going bust. Under the

Labour government, however, some of the older trade unions began to take an increasingly left-of-center position, with increasing support for strikes occurring from time to time. Essentially, however, Britain today is relatively free of the strike action that once plagued the country and the economy. A minimum wage law is now in operation in Britain.

VACATIONS

The average national vacation entitlement is approximately twenty working days (this excludes teachers, who get more), plus the standard public holidays (see Chapter 6). It is accepted that the typical summer vacation will be a maximum of two consecutive weeks, unless a longer period, if available to the employee, has been arranged with the employer beforehand.

The Christmas and New Year period now also tends to extend to two consecutive weeks (outsiders have accused Britain of "closing down" at this time). Many companies now insist that this end-of-year vacation is mandatory, and forms part of the annual holiday entitlement (apart from Christmas Day, Boxing Day, and New Year's Day, which are official public holidays). Covering for absent clerical and administrative colleagues is increasingly required in employment contracts— an exception, perhaps, being the Civil Service.

CONCLUSION

These pages have explored many aspects of the so-called "British" character and what it is to be "British"; but as we have seen, this belies the real truth that it is in its diversity that the "Great" as in "Great Britain" really belongs, never mind its political significance. It is this rich variety that makes Britain what it is today. Extraordinarily, despite the diversity, there exist an overarching feeling of belonging and a sense of common values that give the country its unique character.

It is out of this historical and cultural jigsaw that the British "genius" has evolved: a genius for survival as well as creativity. Against the odds, the monarchy is as popular as ever, the BBC remains the world's most respected public broadcaster, the people's capacity for fair-mindedness, tolerance, and compromise is as strong as ever, and the country is still producing "absent-minded professors" capable of sending a highly sophisticated probe to Mars.

The British continue to be stubborn but courteous, funny but infuriating, friendly but slow to make friends. Britain remains a remarkable and fascinating conundrum—to itself as well as to the outside world.

Further Reading

There is a vast range of books on every conceivable aspect of Britain. Here are a few titles to start with.

Daniel, Christopher. *A Traveller's History—England.* Moreton-in-Marsh: Windrush Press, 1999.

Eagles, Robin. *The Rough Guide History of England.* London: Penguin Books, 2002.

Fox, Kate. *Passport to the Pub: The Tourist's Guide to Pub Etiquette.* London: Brewers and Licensed Retailers Asociation/The Do-Not Press, 1996.

Jackson, Michael. *Malt Whisky Companion.* London: Dorling Kindersley, 1996.

Morgan, Kenneth O. *The Oxford History of Britain.* Oxford: Oxford University Press, 2001.

North, Peter. *Culture Shock! Success Secrets to Maximize Business in Britain.* Singapore: Times Editions, 1999.

Paxman, Jeremy. *The English: A Portrait of a People.* London: Penguin Books, 1999.

Schama, Simon. *A History of Britain* (3 volumes). London: BBC Worldwide, 2000, 2001, 2002.

Tan, Terry. *Culture Shock! Britain. A Guide to Customs and Etiquette.* Portland, Oregon: Graphic Arts Center Publishing, 2000/London: Kuperard, 2003.

Eyewitness Guides London. London: Dorling Kindersley, 1997.

The Green Guide to Scotland. London: Michelin Travel Publications, 2001.

The Green Guide to Wales. London: Michelin Travel Publications, 2001.

Bill Bryson writes about Britain with humor and candor in several of his books, such as *Mother Tongue, Notes from a Small Country,* and *Notes from a Big Country.*

culture smart! **britain**

Index